BESTVINA

Do the Right Thing

A Guide to Christian Morality

James DiGiacomo, S.J.

SHEED & WARD

Franklin, Wisconsin

As an apostolate of the Priests of the Sacred Heart, a Catholic religious order, the mission of Sheed & Ward is to publish books of contemporary impact and enduring merit in Catholic Christian thought and action. The books published, however, reflect the opinion of their authors and are not meant to represent the official position of the Priests of the Sacred Heart.

1991, 1999

Sheed & Ward
7373 South Lovers Lane Road
Franklin, Wisconsin 53132
1-800-266-5564

Printed in the United States of America

Library of Congress Catalog Card Number: 90-61957

ISBN: 1-55612-374-4

2 3 4 5 6 / 02 01 00 99

Contents

1

A Call to Love

A few years ago there was a movie called *Do the Right Thing*. The film, which told the story of an inner city race riot, was a very controversial one that left critics and other viewers arguing for months. This was a lot like real life, because those of us who try to lead decent, upright lives want to do the right thing, but often find ourselves arguing with one another about what is the right thing to do. The arguments only occasionally lead to riots, but they often arouse strong feelings. And sometimes they just leave us confused. It's easy to say "Do the right thing," but it's not always easy to figure out what the right thing is.

Consider, for example, the following cases. They are not true stories, but, as we know from reading the papers or watching the news on TV, or even from personal experience, they are very true to life.

1. I am a highly placed executive in a company that is considering a hostile takeover of another firm. If it goes through, it will mean expanded profits and increased dividends for our shareholders. It will also involve the loss of jobs for several hundred employees, and will not improve service to the public. The move would be legal, but would it be right? Should I support the proposal or oppose it?

2. My mother is 85 years old and has suffered for years from a series of painful and debilitating ailments. A massive stroke has left her in an irreversible coma. Only a respirator and intravenous feeding have kept her alive for the past few weeks; there is no realistic hope of improvement. Should I ask the hospital staff to disconnect the respirator and IVF tubes and let her die in peace?

3. In the coming gubernatorial election in my state, the incumbent governor has vetoed all attempts by the state legislature to re-institute the death penalty, which he considers unjust. The opposing candidate promises to

1

work for the imposition of capital punishment for the most serious crimes. Which candidate is right? How should I vote?

These are just a few of the moral problems that people face from time to time. There are so many more! Should our nation ever use nuclear weapons? Should we even have them? Is it right for two people who love each other to have sexual intercourse if they are not married to each other? If one or both of them are married to someone else? How far may I go to oppose my government's policies in national and international affairs? Is it ever right for me to break the law as part of a protest against injustice? May a childless couple use artificial insemination by a third party in order to have a child?

How do people make up their minds when facing hard choices like these? There are many different ways. Some act decisively from strong personal convictions, while others depend more on the advice of persons whose judgement they respect. Some think it through carefully and logically, others are more inclined to trust their instincts, their gut feelings. Some consider only their own self-interest, while others are more sensitive to the needs and feelings of those who will be affected by their decision. Those who call themselves Christians find guidance, inspiration, and strength in the teachings of Jesus Christ. In his sayings and stories recounted in the New Testament we find the seeds of solutions to some of the most difficult issues facing us, and his example points the way to a just and loving way of life.

If you want to understand Christian morality, however, you must not imagine it as a long list of rules that cover all cases. Think of it rather as a whole way of looking at the world and everyone in it. To Jesus, we are all daughters and sons of one parent, God. This means that *beneath all the differences in race, nationality, education, and age, we are all brothers and sisters in one human family; and in a family there are no strangers*. This is at once the easiest and the hardest truth to grasp. But once we do, we have the key that will unlock some of the most puzzling questions we confront in the matter of right and wrong.

How do we act toward members of our own families? Normally we respect their rights and feelings. We try never to hurt them or treat them unjustly. When we fail, we ask their forgiveness and try to patch things up. More than that, we care about them and feel some responsibility for them. If they are hurting or in need or in trouble, we want to help. If our family is a close and happy one, they know they can count on us and we can count on them. Here we have the basis for Jesus' moral program which we call the Law of Love: "You shall love the Lord your God with your whole heart and soul and strength and mind; and your neighbor as yourself" (Lk 10:27). That's the way good families deal with one another, and that's the way God expects us to act.

Anything that violates the dignity or harms the welfare of another human person is wrong. So is any violation of that person's rights—to life, to health, to property, to reputation. People are not to be used or abused, but treated with fairness and consideration. Not only are we to do them no harm, but we are to look after them, as much as we can, and share responsibility for their welfare. For brothers and sisters are never satisfied with just not hurting one another, but are also concerned about them and willing to care for them. As one writer put it, "Home is where, no matter what you've done, they have to take you in."

It is by this active love of neighbor that we can tell if we love God. Most of us have, at some time, felt like the man who said, "I don't have any problem with God; it's *people* I can't stand!" But, "If anyone says, 'I love God,' and hates his brother, he is a liar; for he who does not love his brother whom he has seen, cannot love God whom he has not seen" (1 Jn 4:20). The true test of our love of God is the way we treat one another.

For many of us, however, this poses a real problem. We all know people whom we dislike intensely, sometimes with good reason. Not only are they not lovable; they seem downright hateful. In our private lives we know people who have wronged us, who have done serious damage to us or to those we love. Are we expected to love those who have robbed us? And on a public level, what about criminals who have committed serious crimes, including cold-blooded murder? Are we supposed to love the international drug dealers who inflict untold human misery and undermine our whole society? The political tyrants who run police states and oppress whole nations?

These are serious objections that must be taken seriously. First of all, *liking* is not the same as *loving*. There will always be some people we just cannot like, no matter how hard we try. (There are probably some who feel the same way about us.) Our feelings are not always subject to our control. It is well to remember that feelings are not right or wrong; they just *are*. What is right or wrong is the way we act on those feelings. Maybe I cannot help disliking someone, but I am still responsible for the way I treat her.

More difficult is the question of those who have committed serious crimes against us or others. We are not expected to close our eyes to evil, or make believe that people are better than they are. It is appropriate for us to feel outrage at crimes committed against persons. What we are asked by God to do is to hate the sin but love the sinner. "You have heard that it was said, 'You shall love your neighbor and hate your enemy.' But I say to you, Love your enemies and pray for those who persecute you, so that you may be sons of your Father who is in heaven; for he makes his sun rise on the evil and on the good, and sends rain on the just and on the unjust" (Mt 5:43-45).

The man who spoke these words in the Sermon on the Mount knew that he was asking us to do something very difficult. So he died on the cross for everyone, including the worst sinners among us. In Christ we have someone who not only calls us to greatness but shows the way. He doesn't stop at setting us an example, either. He knows that such virtue is beyond our strength, so he does not leave us alone. He promises that his grace will never be lacking, that we will always have the help we need to attain the ideal that he sets before us. "I have said this to you, that in me you may have peace. In the world you have tribulation; but be of good cheer, I have overcome the world" (Jn. 16:33).

So far, so good. But one day a man pushed Jesus one step further, asking, "And who is my neighbor?" He answered with the well-known story of the Good Samaritan. A man who had been robbed and beaten lay by the side of the road. Two of his countrymen passed him by; they didn't want to get involved. But a Samaritan went out of his way to give him the help that he needed. And so the expression "Good Samaritan" came into our language. But you must understand that, to the people Jesus told this story, the Samaritans were a hated minority. As far as many of them were concerned, the only good Samaritan was a dead Samaritan. Maybe the hero of the story didn't like Jews either, but that day he overcame his feelings and saw only a fellow human being who needed help. In telling the story this way, Jesus makes his fellow Jews look bad. He implicitly condemns the priest and the Levite, not for anything they did, but for what they failed to do. They failed to love.

What is Jesus saying to you and me in this story? It is clear that by "love of neighbor" he is not talking about a vague feeling of good will or just "being nice." He's talking about *action*. If someone needs me, I'm supposed to *do* something. This is a challenging way of thinking about morality; it doesn't come easily to most of us. Love of God and neighbor means more than warm feelings, more than avoiding the breaking of rules. It means living up to the responsibility we normally feel toward those who are closest to us, and extending that love to all of God's children without exception. That's a big order! To do this, we have to stop thinking of people in terms of "us" and "them." If we are serious about following Christ, we must try to stop dividing people up into two groups, those we should care about and those who don't matter.

This is what makes Christian morality different: it tells us to care about *everybody*. It rejects all kinds of tribalism, the tendency we all have to narrow the scope of our concern to one family, one group, one gender, one race, one nation. Ask any ten people what they would do if they found a wallet. Some of them would keep it, some would return it, and some would say, "it depends." On what? "If I knew the owner." It is normal for us to think one way about people who are like us, and another way about those who are different. Racism, sexism, and nationalism are so common that they seem almost natural. But Christians are not supposed to settle for what is "normal" or "natural." In Jesus' words, we are called up "to be perfect, as our heavenly Father is Perfect" (Mt. 5:48). Since God loves and watches over all creatures without exception, so must we.

Does this mean that we must have exactly the same kinds of love for all people? Not really. Those who are closest to us, such as spouses, children, and blood relations, have first call on our love and care. The poor, the helpless, and the vulnerable also have a special right to our concern. But in making different moral choices the key question must always be: How will this affect my sisters and brothers in the larger human family? Will my decision respect their dignity, their rights, their welfare?

Jesus' law of love does not immediately provide simple answers to all the difficult moral problems that people face from time to time. But it does give us a way to approach them and maybe find our way through the confusion. The rest of this book will deal with several of the most urgent issues in detail, as we work together to find solutions that we can live with in good conscience.

Questions of right and wrong touch all of life, not just special parts. Say "immorality" to some people, and they immediately think you're talking about sex. But morality is much bigger than that. God's command to do good and avoid evil concerns the way people do business. It touches the actions of doctors and nurses, their patients and their families. It has a lot to say about personal relationships, about marriages and about family life.

God takes great interest in the way we wage war and the way we make peace. The way we treat our environment, and the condition in which we leave the earth to our children. In immigration policies and voting rights and zoning regulations and tax structures. For all of these have a great impact on the welfare of God's daughters and sons.

So morality is a social as well as a personal matter. It concerns not only the way individuals treat one another but also the way larger groups, companies, and whole societies behave. It includes the economic and political policies engaged in by governments and nations. For the rights, the welfare, and even the lives of people are affected not only by the actions of individuals but even more by the social structures of whole peoples. All of these institutions are subject to moral judgement. And each of us is responsible not only for the way our individual actions affect others, but for the impact we have as members of economic, social and political systems.

Some of us may find this way of thinking about morality unfamiliar and uncomfortable. For example, we may think of politics and economics as activities outside morality, which is, it seems, a purely private and personal concern. Thus politics is seen as having its own rules, which concern getting elected and passing and enforcing legislation, and as having nothing to do with personal morality. Likewise, the rules of the marketplace, such as the laws of supply and demand, are considered off limits to criticism in terms of right and wrong. So long as no laws are broken, we feel, we need not bother ourselves with added "moral" questions. All that matters is the "bottom line." In the conduct of foreign policy, all we want to know is whether our country's interests are served. People who think this way about economics and national and international politics are sometimes called *pragmatists.* They ask not whether a policy is right or wrong but simply whether it is effective: *Does it work?* That's all they have to know.

Christians, on the other hand, can never be satisfied with this way of thinking, for reasons which should already be quite clear. People's lives, their welfare, and their dignity are affected not only by the behavior of individuals but also by the laws and policies of governments, banks, and companies. What stockholders call "good business" may not always be good for people. What governments do in the name of "national security" may sometimes violate basic human rights. Jesus once said that laws were made for people, and not people for laws. Those who follow him insist that all such practises are subject to moral review. As the Second Vatican Council states, "Those people are wrong who think that religion consists in acts of worship alone and in the discharge of certain moral obligations, and who imagine that they can plunge themselves into earthly affairs as if to imply that these are altogether divorced from the religious life. This split between the faith which many profess and their daily lives deserves to be counted among the most serious errors of our age" (*Pastoral Constitution on the Church in the Modern World*).

Still, some are not convinced. They say that applying moral principles to political and economic questions violates the principle of separation of church and state. There are several points of confusion here.

The First Amendment to the Constitution of the United States declares that in this country there is to be no official religion. This means that, unlike most other nations at the time this country was founded, there is to be no established church. No religion is to receive special privileges, and people are not to be penalized for not belonging to a particular church. They are free to profess any religion, or no religion at all. At the time of this nation's founding, this was an unusual arrangement; since then, it has become quite common around the world. Some Americans wrongly conclude that since the State is neutral toward all religions and churches, religion must be a completely private matter with no influence on public life. But the Constitution says no such thing.

The second point of confusion concerns the relation between morality and religion. In the minds of many, they are the same thing; but of course they are not. While it is true that most churchgoers get their ideas of right and wrong from their religious backgrounds, there are also people who belong to no religion at all but still have strong moral convictions. You don't have to belong to a religion, or go to a church, or even believe in God to know that stealing and murder are wrong. There are atheists and agnostics who fight for justice in public and private life. In the last century, some Abolitionists who led the struggle against slavery were people of no particular religious faith. In this century, so were some of the leaders of the Civil Rights movement. They fought side by side with religious and churchgoing Americans for the same thing—liberty and justice for all.

Morality and religion, then, are often connected in the minds and hearts of people; but they are two different things. So when Americans try to apply principles of morality to political and economic issues, they are not trying to impose their religious beliefs on their fellow citizens. They are simply working for a more just society, in which standards of fairness and decency prevail.

The first followers of Jesus Christ did not immediately call themselves Christians. That title would come later. The first name for their movement recorded in the New Testament is "The Way." Before they carefully worked out the expression and development of doctrine, they called themselves the people of the Way. They saw themselves as committed to a life of action in imitation of their Lord and Savior. "There was not a needy person among them, for as many as were possessors of lands or houses sold them, and brought the proceeds of what was sold and laid it at the apostles' feet; and distribution was made to each as any had need" (Acts 4:34).

These were people who cared about one another and saw their faith in Christ as binding them together into one loving family. We know from other New Testament readings that they had many problems and disputes, as do all families; but they worked them out together in terms of justice and love. Indeed, we read that they made a tremendous impression on the men and women of their time: "See the Christians, how they love one another!" Their religion was not just morality, but it was the moral quality of their lives that made them stand out. And so it must be with us.

Today we confront moral problems that the early Christians never even dreamt of. Our world is so much more sophisticated than theirs: Developments in modern medicine, technology, weapons and communications both enrich and complicate our lives. But the principles by which we live are the same as theirs. Our principles are based on the same values that they learned from Jesus Christ. Love of God and neighbor, respect for all God's children, and commitment to the welfare of all members of God's family must govern the way we make judgements of right and wrong as well as the crucial decisions that affect our lives and the lives of others. The rest of this book will try to put those principles and values to work in facing the hard questions that challenge us to express our faith in deeds of justice and love.

2

Feeling Good and Being Good

Making moral judgements and decisions would often be difficult even if we could agree on the answers to the hard questions. But one of the most striking features of our society is the lack of agreement on many of the most fundamental issues that face us. Americans are divided on capital punishment, sexual equality, abortion, nuclear weapons, homosexuality, euthanasia, and marriage, to name just a few. The disagreements are numerous and deep, and they cut across lines of education, intelligence, and even religion. They concern not only particular issues but the very roots of morality, the way we should decide on matters of right and wrong. That is why some of the most intelligent and earnest people oppose us even when we are following our deepest personal convictions.

Why are we so divided? Why can't people of obvious good will see eye to eye on the most basic moral issues? One of the reasons for so much quarreling is our inability to agree on what we are looking for. For some people, moral questioning is a search for truth, while for others it is just a matter of taste. The second group feels that labeling actions as "right" and "wrong" is really just a matter of opinion, and that one opinion is as good as another. As far as they're concerned, it's all a matter of how you look at it. Or, as the expression goes, "morality is in the eye of the beholder." From this point of view, when we call some things right or wrong, we're not saying how they *are* but rather how we *see* them. And if you and I see things differently, there is no way to settle the argument. Indeed, there is no sense in carrying on the dispute, because we are just arguing about matters of taste. You have your opinion, and I have mine.

People who think about morality this way are called *relativists*. When asked about some moral question, for example, "is extramarital sex right?," they will probably say something like, "If you think it's right, it's right for you. But if someone else thinks it's wrong, then it's wrong for that person. But neither one can say what's right or wrong for the other, because it's all relative."

Once you accept this way of thinking, certain familiar attitudes and ways of speaking are bound to follow. If Jane thinks abortion is wrong but Marie thinks it's alright, then Jane may refrain from abortion; but if Marie is having an abortion, Jane has no right to tell her that she's doing something wrong. She would be seen as "imposing her morality" on Marie, and this would be quite unreasonable, since the relativist sees morality as a game in which each of the players makes his or her own truth. In other words, it's a purely private matter, and for some people to tell others that they are doing something wrong is to violate their privacy.

This also explains why most people who favor abortion do not call themselves "pro-abortion" but rather "pro-choice." They say that it is alright for people to object to abortion on moral grounds, as long as they don't interfere with the freedom of choice of those who disagree with them. As you can see, what they are saying is that if *I* choose to have an abortion, then it's right *for me. My* moral choices are right for *me*, as long as I make them *freely*.

Attractive but Absurd

This way of looking at moral questions is evidently very appealing, since so many people of our time think and talk this way. "Freedom" and "privacy" are dear to the hearts of all Americans, and they should be. After all, there are many places in the world where these rights are not respected, so that people suffer great injustices. We do well to insist on freedom and privacy and to resist any attempts to limit their exercise.

However, the idea of not passing judgement on people and letting them follow their preferences does have its limitations. If we fail to recognize these, we may find ourselves defending some rather absurd positions. A simple example makes this clear. Thieves exercise their freedom of choice by robbing people. When the police catch them, we impose our morality on them by putting them behind bars. We do the same to rapists and embezzlers and murderers. We punish them for exercising their freedom of choice in ways that violate the rights of other persons to life or property.

So the moral relativists are not completely consistent in the way they make their judgements. Of course not. They are just as sensitive and caring as others, and they know that we have to take a stand somewhere. Some crimes are so obvious that they must be condemned and punished. Still, they are left with the question: *why* are some actions clearly wrong, while others are just a matter of opinion? Some relativists would answer by pointing out that rape, embezzlement and murder are different from abortion in that they are illegal. But this is not a satisfactory answer, because it confuses *morality* with *legality*. It implies that if something is permitted by law then it is morally right; and that if something is forbidden by law, then it is morally wrong.

At first sight this seems quite reasonable. After all, don't we make laws against certain actions because we look upon them as wrong? Of course. And they nearly always are. But not always. We know from history and from observation that sometimes laws are unjust. They may penalize people for doing what is right, or allow people to violate human rights and get away with it.

A few examples immediately come to mind. In Nazi Germany it was legal to murder Jews and other "undesirables," and illegal to shelter them from the police. But no one today would say that it was right to murder innocent people or that it was wrong to hide them from their murderers. Similarly, in the southern United States in the last century, it was legal to buy and sell slaves, and illegal to help them escape from their masters. But the slaveowners, whether they realized it or not, were doing something wrong, and the people who ran the underground railway were doing something right. Moreover, slavery did not become wrong only after President Lincoln signed the Emancipation Proclamation and made it illegal. It was *always* wrong, and the law finally recognized it. That's the *truth* of the matter. The practise of slavery and the Nazi holocaust were wrong, and nothing could ever make them right. These were not matters of taste but of truth.

In order, then, to settle the question of the morality of abortion, we must distinguish between legality and morality. We have to talk about matters other than freedom and privacy. We have to ask what abortion is. Does it violate the right to life of innocent persons? Later in this book we will examine the abortion issue in greater detail. Here we are using it only as an example of how to make a moral judgement. In this and in other issues we must ask not only whether people are acting freely but what it is that they are doing. When we face difficult questions like "Is it right to practise euthanasia to end a person's suffering?" we must find out not only whether people are acting freely or sincerely, but what it is that they are doing. Specifically, are they respecting the dignity and rights of other persons or are they violating them?

Does It Work?

Similar to the philosophy of moral relativism is that of *pragmatism.* Moral pragmatists may not be consciously relativistic, but they have a hard time figuring out *why* things should be considered right or wrong, so they settle for the rule of thumb: Does it work? Ask pragmatists the source of the values or convictions on which they ground their commitments, and they will usually say something like, "I can't speak for others, but these values seem to work for me. In pursuing them I find a sense of satisfaction; when I achieve them, I feel good about myself."

Some of the most earnest and well-meaning people talk this way. They genuinely want to do what is right. But because they are consciously or unconsciously relativistic, they have reduced the whole notion of *being* good to *feeling* good. Like relativists, they measure morality not by any standard distinct from themselves but simply by their own feelings about themselves. In trying to make up their minds about how to act in some difficult moral matter, they ask not "Is it right?," but, "Do I feel comfortable with this course of action?" Once again, each person becomes the maker of his or her own moral truth. Because you feel differently about some ways of acting, your truth is different from mine; so we are unable to share convictions or values or commitments. We are left with nothing but the lonely privacy of individual human beings with no truth to share, each in our own little self-justifying world. You do your thing, and I'll do mine. We can never criticize or call each other to something better. We can only leave each other alone.

Ernest Hemingway once defined morality this way: "Right" is what you feel good about after you've done it; "wrong" is what you feel bad about having done. There is a certain wisdom and a limited truth in this statement, but it also has some serious limitations. There are robbers who, after pulling off a successful crime, feel very good afterwards. They give one another high fives as they split up the loot. There are some people who use sex only to manipulate others and dominate them and then discard them. After such sexual conquests, they typically feel quite proud of themselves. What they _should feel is_ guilty, because they have done something wrong. The successful criminal's morality "works" for him, so long as he stays out of jail. But even then, he is a twisted human being and a menace to society, buying his sense of well-being at the expense of innocent people whose rights he has violated. He feels good, but he's no good. Our feelings, then, are not always the best clues to whether we have acted properly.

Follow Your Conscience

All these considerations should help us to understand what is meant by the expression, "follow your conscience." On one level, the meaning is very clear. You should do what you think is right, and refrain from doing what you think is wrong. "Conscience" describes an act of the mind whereby I make a judgement about the rightness or wrongness of an action. If I find a wallet with money, credit cards and the owner's name, address, and phone number, I ask myself, "Is it right for me to keep it? Or should I return wallet and money to the owner?" If, in my judgement, it is wrong to keep it, my conscience is telling me to call up the owner. If I follow through and call her up, I have followed my conscience; i.e., I have done what I thought was right.

On the other hand, suppose I manage to convince myself that I have a right to the wallet. "Finders, keepers." "It's her own fault for losing it; I don't owe her anything." In this case, my conscience is telling me that it's alright to keep the wallet. If I do, I am, again, following my conscience.

But I am doing something _wrong_. That wallet doesn't belong to me, and I have no right to it. The owner doesn't lose her right to her property just because she cannot now see it.

You can see, from these examples, that "following your conscience" does not guarantee that you will do the right thing. This raises the question of how we _form_ our conscience. How do I go about deciding whether something is right or wrong? Do I ask whether it's legal? Whether I can get away with it? How much I could buy with the money? Whether I have any right to another's property? If you put this case to many young people, they will answer, "I'd return it if I knew the owner; otherwise, I'd keep it."

But this is a tribalistic solution. It says, in effect, that people who are known to me have rights, but strangers don't.

Where many people go wrong is in assuming that if they just follow their conscience, they're sure to do the right thing. Of course there is no guarantee of this. All of us, at some time or another, have talked ourselves into doing things that we should have realized were wrong. Under the influence of fear or greed or selfishness or some other unworthy motive, we are capable of convincing ourselves of many things when we ought to know better.

And yet there is a sense in which the saying is absolutely true: I am obliged to follow my conscience. God does not judge me on whether I always do what is, in fact, the right thing. (Thank heaven for that!) Because God knows how difficult it is sometimes, in a moral issue, to arrive at the truly correct solution; and that honest, sincere people sometimes arrive at the wrong conclusions through no fault of their own. What God does insist on is that I do my very best to form my conscience correctly, to find the truth, and then to follow my deepest personal convictions.

Forming Conscience

How should we form our conscience? Well, first of all, we should follow Hemingway's rule and listen to our feelings. They are not infallible, as we have seen, but they are often a good indicator of whether we are acting as we should. Then, as in any important matter, we should get the best advice we can. This may mean consulting a friend whose judgement we respect, or reading something by an acknowledged expert on the matter in question. It may mean reading the Bible attentively and prayerfully, seeking guidance in God's word, especially in the teachings of Jesus. And Catholics can gain enlightenment from the teachings of their church. Bishops in union with the Pope exercise a special ministry of teaching in matters of faith and morals as part of their role as spiritual leaders. They can be a big help to anyone who seeks help in making difficult moral decisions. Indeed, they are an authority that Catholics may not simply ignore and still consider themselves faithful members of their church. Last but not least, we should pray to God for help, so that we may know what to do and have the strength to do it.

In order to go about forming our conscience this way, we need a healthy sense of our own limitations. We must recognize that we can deceive ourselves about what is right and wrong, especially when we stand to gain or lose something important by our decisions. We need a mature person's understanding of what real freedom is: not a license to do whatever we please, but the ability to search for the truth no matter where it leads. All this demands more than intelligence. It calls for courage, unselfishness, humility, and integrity. That is why the smartest or the most educated people are not always the most virtuous, and why some who were neither brilliant nor cultivated have become great saints.

The Authoritarian Short Cut

In the course of this chapter, we have shown that it is not enough simply to exercise our freedom of choice without examining the effects of our choices on others as well as ourselves. We have pointed out how dangerous it is to trust our consciences without being careful to form them by study, consultation, and prayer.

There is another kind of error which lies at the other end of the scale so to speak. Some persons are so intimidated by the complexity of moral issues, so aware of their own limitations and their inability to solve moral questions, that they stop trying to figure them out. Instead they choose some authority figure, and give it total, unqualified obedience. By presuming that the authority is infallible, they hope to be sure of not making mistakes.

This kind of approach to moral decision making, which we may call *authoritarianism*, takes many different forms. One disturbing example is that of religious cults. Here the members surrender all individuality and leave all decisions about their life and work to the cult leader. Some explain this behavior as the result of "brainwashing;" others interpret it as the fulfillment of some temporary psychological need for security. Another form of authoritarianism turns up in military life, where some officers demand total, unquestioning obedience and some soldiers are quite ready to give it. "Ours not to reason why, ours but to do and die." Some citizens see the nation as such an authority figure, especially in time of war. They both give and demand blind obedience: "My country, right or wrong!" "Love it or leave it."

In each of these cases the individual has decided that the only way to act correctly is to surrender all personal responsibility to a leader or to an institution. This is done in the name of loyalty or obedience. Such total submission has sometimes inspired heroic bravery and self-sacrifice; that's the good news. But there's bad news as well, as recent history has taught us. In Guyana in 1978, 900 members of a cult committed mass suicide at the command of a mad, charismatic leader. Following World War II, the War Crimes trials at Nuremburg gave us the spectacle of defendants justifying unspeakable atrocities by insisting that they were only following orders. During the Vietnam war, Americans were shocked and outraged when they learned of the Mylai massacre. Our soldiers had systematically murdered hundreds of unarmed, helpless Vietnamese villagers, most of whom were old men, women, and children. The only reason they gave for this senseless slaughter was that they were obeying orders. As a result of such incidents, many people today are suspicious of authoritarianism and are convinced that individuals must never completely surrender their freedom. In forming our conscience, we must never give blind obedience but rather exercise judgement and take responsibility for our actions. Authority should assist conscience, not replace it.

Avoiding Extremes

What do we learn from this brief look at the different ways in which people make moral decisions? We can better understand why as a people we are so divided. We disagree not only on particular issues but on the very way we should approach them. At one extreme, *relativists* and *pragmatists* despair of ever finding the truth, and concentrate only on their own private feelings about the way they should act. At the other extreme, *authoritarians* give up their personal judgement and surrender all responsibility to someone else. As Christians we must resist the temptation to settle for either of these extremes. Against the relativists, we insist that the moral life is a search for truth. Unlike the pragmatists, we believe that there is more to being good than feeling good. Against the authoritarians, we insist that truly adult persons must take responsibility for their lives and hence must respect the dignity of personal conscience. But that conscience does not function in a vacuum; it must be carefully formed with the help of others, especially those who teach in the name of Christ.

This is the way Jesus himself lived and taught. He never talked about right and wrong as if they were just a matter of opinion. He respected the freedom of his hearers, but he spoke out boldly against injustice and told people who were doing wrong to stop it. He obeyed his country's laws but warned that we must never give to Caesar what belongs to God. He respected the religious authorities of his day but reminded them that laws were made for people, not the other way around. Thus he showed us how to face the hard choices. He doesn't give us easy answers, but he helps us find the truth in a time of confusion when many well-meaning people have lost their way.

3

At Life's Beginning

The birth of a child has always been a time of anticipation, anxiety, and joy. New advances in medicine and in reproductive technology have brought new possibilities, new choices, and sometimes agonizing decisions to be made. The events leading up to and surrounding birth have always been an awesome experience for parents, giving them the feeling of being in touch, in a special way, with the mystery of life. But recent developments have removed much of the mystery and given us greater control over the conceiving and bearing of children. How should we use this new power?

Consider some of the relatively recent developments in child-bearing. Childless couples can now resort to artificial insemination, surrogate mothers, or *in vitro* fertilization and "test tube" babies. During pregnancy they can monitor the development of the fetus through the use of amniocentesis or sonograms. Intrauterine medicine is a development that may be just around the corner. And newborns with severe birth defects who would have perished a few years ago can now be kept alive. These advances have both a positive and a negative side. They bring wonderful benefits but also raise some very difficult moral questions.

Consider, first of all, some of the new ways of having children. For couples who, because of sterility or other physical problems, are unable to have children in the normal way, the new reproductive technology seems at first sight like the answer to their prayers. But is it right for a husband and wife to employ the sperm or egg of a third party and thus have a child who is begotten by only one of the spouses? Should children be conceived not by an act of loving intimacy but by artificial clinical techniques? The monitoring of fetal development is, in itself, a positive advantage. But amniocentesis poses a slight but real danger to the life of the unborn; is it justified? And both amniocentesis and the sonogram are often employed with an eye to a possible abortion if they reveal diseases or other handicaps in the developing child. Even the ability to save the lives of infants with severe birth defects is not an unmixed blessing. Sometimes the means of sustaining life in these cases are accompanied by such severe suffering that we wonder if it is right to impose such burdens in order to ensure survival. And sometimes the kind of life that is available to these tiny sufferers makes parents wonder if it is really a gift to be preserved at all costs.

New Methods of Conception

As in most other moral questions, Americans are divided in their opinion of these new methods of reproduction. For *relativists*, the question is simply one of free choice. As long as artificial insemination, surrogate wombs and even sperm banks are legal, there is no problem; and they will oppose any attempt to restrict these practises in any way. The *pragmatists*, as usual, feel pretty much the same way. All they want to know is, do the new methods work? The way they see it, any man or woman who wants a child has a right to one, however that child may be conceived. If we can do it, then it's OK.

Christians, however, have grave moral reservations about some of these methods. The most serious objection arises from Christian teaching about marriage and the family. Following the teachings of Jesus, his followers consider marriage to be a sacred union in God's eyes. Any participation by a third party through artificial insemination or surrogate womb violates that unity and is an attack on the integrity of the family; in effect, it is the same as adultery. Children are seen as a gift of God bestowed on two people who are permanently and exclusively committed to each other and their family. Children should come into being as the result of the love of mother and father.

Christians are not the only ones who consider some of these reproductive methods immoral. For example, the use of sperm banks is seen by many as an irresponsible and unworthy way of being a parent. Anonymous donors contribute their sperm to be used in the artificial insemination of women who are either married to sterile husbands or are not married but choose to be single parents. Such arrangements are objectionable for several reasons. The *biological father* takes no responsibility for his children, since he does not even know them. Parenthood is reduced to the mere exercise of a biological function. The *married woman* who uses a third party's sperm violates the unity of her family. And the *single woman* deprives her child of the committed love of a caring father. Finally, there is the more notorious example of the *surrogate mother*, which needs to be examined in some detail.

The Case of Baby M

The most famous case of surrogate parenting is that of William and Elizabeth Stern and Mary Beth Whitehead. Because Elizabeth Stern was unable to give her husband a child, they engaged the services of Mrs. Whitehead who agreed to be artificially inseminated by Dr. Stern. She signed a contract for $10,000 and agreed to surrender the child at birth. During pregnancy and after giving birth to a little girl known as Baby M, or Melissa, Mrs. Whitehead became very attached to the child and refused to give her up. The Sterns sued and won a court judgement which gave them sole custody and allowed Elizabeth (Stern) to adopt the child. The verdict was appealed and the judgement reversed by the New Jersey Supreme Court. By this verdict, the Sterns were again given custody, but Elizabeth Stern was denied the right to adopt. The rights of Mary Beth Whitehead as the child's natural mother were upheld, and the three adults were ordered to work out arrangements for regular visitation between mother and child. The Court also declared that such surrogate parent contracts stipulating payment of money were henceforth illegal in New Jersey.

Although this decision of the New Jersey Supreme Court deals with legality and not morality, it points up several aspects of the case that help us to make moral judgements on the practise of surrogate parenthood. Although neither Mary Beth Whitehead nor the Sterns thought of it this way when they were making the contract, what they were engaged in was a clear case of baby-selling. They thought of it simply as payment for a service rendered, but, in fact, Baby M was for sale. Moreover, in contracts of this kind, we usually have poor women bearing children for the rich. Perhaps worst of all, women are being sought to bear children whom they, in effect, promise not to love. When someone like Mary Beth Whitehead realizes that she loves her child and cannot just give her up because she has signed a piece of paper, she learns from bitter personal experience how profoundly unnatural this arrangement is. Indeed, she feels this so strongly that she has joined other surrogate mothers like herself in a public campaign to mobilize people against entering such agreements. Even when no money changes hands, women are arranging to surrender their children and renounce all responsibility for them. This is fooling with Nature, with a vengeance, and the price in human terms is unacceptably high. Worst of all, it is a failure to care for those who have first call on our love and concern—our own children.

A Possible Exception

There is one kind of case involving new methods of conception which has received differing reactions in the Catholic community. May a husband and wife use *in vitro* fertilization which does not involve a third party? The child is truly theirs, since *his* sperm and *her* egg are joined, though artificially. On one hand, the 1987 Vatican Declaration rejected this method of conception as an artificial intrusion into married life. On the other hand, some respected theologians and many married people, believe that such intervention is justified, since it takes place within the family and makes it possible for a couple to have a child. As one theologian put it, "not everything artificial is unnatural." This is the only significant disagreement among Catholic thinkers on the subject of reproductive technology.

Let us now consider the difficult decisions that face parents of children with severe birth defects. Sometimes these come to light even before birth, when prenatal examination reveals some diseases and deformities. Some parents then choose to have an abortion. This cannot be justified, however, since the unborn child has a right to life despite its sickness or handicap. Those who urge abortion try to justify their course by arguing that the child will not enjoy a decent quality of life. But this is a shallow way to estimate the value of a human life. It says, in effect, that only the healthy, the beautiful, and the perfect have a right to live. It is discriminatory against the weak, the helpless, and the infirm who are also made in God's image and share in the dignity and rights of all of God's children. They deserve to be loved and cared for, not devalued and rejected.

When couples consider monitoring the condition of an unborn child through amniocentesis or sonogram, they should be clear about why they are doing it. If the purpose is to ascertain the child's condition and prepare to give special care after birth if needed, this is good medical practise. But if the purpose is to gain information that will help them decide whether to have an abortion, then it is not justified. For then we are not aiming at the good of the child but are considering the option of doing it harm by taking its life. Someday intrauterine medicine may become a reality, and then prenatal diagnosis will be the prelude to treatment and healing. But that may still be many years away.

The Case of Infant Doe

A baby boy known only as Infant Doe was born in a Bloomington, Indiana hospital in 1982. The child was born with two strikes against him. He had Downes Syndrome and his esophagus was not connected to his stomach. Nothing could be done about the Downes Syndrome condition, which would cause an unknown degree of retardation. The disconnected esophagus was immediately life-threatening; if not repaired, it would cause death in a few days. The operation was major but not unusual, and had good odds of success. One of the attending physicians, over the protests of a colleague, advised the parents that since a poor quality of life awaited the infant, they did not have to approve the surgery. They agreed and refused to allow the operation, in effect condemning the baby to death by starvation. While advocates for the child sought a court order to mandate the operation, several couples in the area offered to adopt and raise the child. The parents were steadfast in their refusal, and before the courts could act the child died.

When this case became public knowledge, it caused widespread disputes and outraged protests around the country. Some were sympathetic to the parents. Either they accepted the "quality of life" argument and agreed that the Downes Syndrome child was better off dead, or they defended the parents' decision as a matter of privacy—the "freedom of choice" argument with which we are familiar. Others condemned the action of the parents and the hospital as an act of murder by starvation, brought on by gross discrimination against a handicapped person. Before the furor subsided, the federal government imposed strict new regulations, known as "Baby Doe Rules," on hospitals to ensure fair treatment of infants with birth defects.

In some ways this was a difficult decision for the parents. One can indeed sympathize with them as they faced the prospect of caring for a Downes Syndrome child. Fear, anxiety, confusion and guilt contributed to their part in the tragedy. But the moral duty of everyone involved is clear. Infant Doe, whose only crime was in being a "special child," had an inalienable right to life which was violated by withholding treatment. The sad story of his short life should alert us to our duty to protect the weak and helpless in a society which glorifies beauty and power and looks down on those who lack them as "unproductive" and hence without value or dignity. Some commentators on this case also pointed out that, if the parents were unable to care for Infant Doe, then society (which is another name for all of us) had a duty to provide that care.

The Case of Baby Jane Doe

A case somewhat like that of Infant Doe but significantly different and more difficult was that of a girl known as Baby Jane Doe, born in a Long Island (N.Y.) hospital in 1983. Her medical problems were many and serious. She suffered from spina bifida (an open spinal column), hydrocephalus (excessive fluid on the brain), microcephaly (unusually small head) and malformation of the brain stem. The little girl's parents were faced with two choices, both of them heartbreaking. She could have major surgery to correct the spinal condition; this was a dangerous, life-threatening operation. If successful, it would probably enable her to live a painful, bedridden life accompanied by continued medical complications, possible further operations, with a maximum life expectancy of twenty years. Or they could forgo the surgery and give her conventional care and therapy. In this case, she would live with fewer complications and more comfortably, but she would probably die by the age of two.

After listening to advice not only from medical experts but also from clergy, and after serious prayer and reflection, the parents chose the second course of action. They were convinced that this would be in the best interests of their child. Many, but not all, agreed with their decision. Some thought that they should have done everything they could to gain as long a life as possible for Baby Jane Doe. They felt that her parents were acting like Infant Doe's parents in Bloomington, depriving her of a chance at a longer life to avoid the burden of bringing up a severely handicapped child. They reasoned that Baby Jane had a right to all the medical resources that were available, and that this right was being violated.

Others, however, defended the parents' choice with arguments that were both bad and good. The bad arguments are familiar ones, based on privacy and quality of life. They reasoned that it was a private decision of the parents and no one else's business. But the way parents treat their children is not a purely private matter; if it were, society would not intervene in cases of abuse and neglect. Or they argued that since the child would have a poor quality of life it was not worth protecting. We have seen how this line of thought is unjust because it is prejudiced against handicapped children and considers them and their lives as worthless.

But these were not the grounds on which Baby Jane's parents made their hard choice. Negatively, they decided against risking her life through radical surgery. Positively, they preferred the treatment that would make her short life as comfortable and free of suffering as possible. If this meant fewer years of life, it would still be of greater benefit to her because it would lessen the burden of suffering. And she would be given all the love and care they could provide.

Burden and Benefit

This is the kind of difficult case about which good and intelligent people can and do disagree. Perhaps there is not one single answer that can settle the dispute. But two terms emerge that enable parents, physicians and moralists to deal with other similar dilemmas: *burden* and *benefit*. In deciding on how to treat newborn children with serious birth defects, we should ask these two questions: 1) How great a burden of suffering or danger will the proposed treatments impose on the child? 2) What benefit may result? The burden and benefit must then be compared. Is the possible or probable benefit great enough to justify putting the patient through this risk or suffering? This is not like a mathematical formula that produces a single, clear answer. But it is a responsible way to approach difficult problems. It often helps us to reach solutions that make sense and reassure us that we are acting in the patient's best interests.

Baby Jane Doe's parents decided that the benefits that might result from dangerous surgery were not great enough to justify the risks. It was a good decision. If Infant Doe's parents had applied the same principle, they might have concluded that the operation to connect her esophagus and stomach was well worth it, since the benefit to be achieved was survival and a chance at meaningful life.

When we apply this principle to other difficult cases, we can come up with answers that satisfy our moral sense and also do justice to the parties concerned. Take, for example, the case of anencephalic infants, who lack all or a major part of the brain. Heroic, ingenious, and expensive measures can be taken to keep them alive, but they will never be able to achieve consciousness or interact with people around them. There is life here, but is it *human* life? This is one of those instances where the burden of treatment falls heavily upon parents and drains available medical resources to no one's benefit. Treatment here is useless. It is clearly a time to admit defeat and to accept the fact that sometimes we should not do everything we can.

Preventive Measures

Up to now we have been discussing what parents and physicians should do for infants who have been born with serious defects or who have been detected before birth as being in serious difficulties. Is there any way to foresee these problems and prevent them from happening?

Although many of these tragic dilemmas are impossible to anticipate, some can be headed off beforehand. Spouses with certain genetic configurations run a high risk of conceiving seriously defective children. This usually comes to light after the birth of a child afflicted with a congenital disease, but sometimes the family history of one or both spouses flashes danger signs. Genetic counselors can then inform spouses of the odds of their giving birth to handicapped offspring. It is the obligation of parents to make use of these services and to consider together what their responsibilities are. If they run a very high risk of begetting children with very debilitating ailments, they must ask themselves and each other: Is it right to bring a child into the world in such conditions? Some deformities are so devastating that we may honestly question whether such a life can still be called a gift.

There is no one simple answer for all spouses at genetic risk, but the questions should not be avoided. We owe it to our children not only to do all we can to cure their ills, but to try to prevent ills as well. This may sometimes lead us to the painful conclusion that the most loving thing is not to bring them into the world at all.

This whole chapter has tried to deal, in a carefully reasoned way, with situations that are usually emotionally draining. As in most human crises, the heart has reasons which the head cannot always comprehend. But emotions can also cloud our understanding and work against sound judgement. In their desire to have children, men and women should not resort to means that are enticing but unworthy. In the face of severe birth defects, they should resist the temptation to deprive the innocent of life. At the other extreme, they should not feel obligated to take futile measures that impose unreasonable burdens on their children or themselves.

The Verdict on Baby M

"The surrogacy contract violates the policy of this State that the rights of natural parents are equal concerning their child, the father's right no greater than the mother's . . . The whole purpose and effect of the surrogacy contract was to give the father the exclusive right to the child by destroying the rights of the mother.

"Under the contract, the natural mother is irrevocably committed before she knows the strength of her bond with her child. She never makes a totally voluntary, informed decision, for quite clearly any decision prior to the baby's birth is, in the most important sense, uninformed, and any decision after that, compelled by a pre-existing contractual commitment, the threat of a lawsuit, and the inducement of a $10,000 payment, is less than totally voluntary. Her interests are of little concern to those who controlled this transaction. . . . Worst of all, however, is the contract's total disregard of the best interests of the child. There is not the slightest suggestion that any inquiry will be made at any time to determine the fitness of the Sterns as custodial parents, of Mrs. Stern as an adoptive parent, or the effect on the child of not living with her natural mother.

"This is the sale of a child, or, at the very least, the sale of a mother's right to her child, the only mitigating factor being that one of the purchasers is the father. Almost every evil that prompted the prohibition of the payment of money in connection with adoption exists here."

—From the decision of the New Jersey Supreme Court
invalidating the Baby M contract

Defending the Defenseless

"The pragmatic spirit of America has serious consequences for the way in which we come to value persons, most especially the sick, elderly, poor, handicapped, and the unborn. In our up and doing society, which glorifies the Pepsi Generation, we have little patience and value for those who don't, can't or won't make a social contribution. We come to value persons in terms of status, power, and social worth. American society rewards those who have the ability to produce and consume. The television media holds up for us images and models who display economic clout and are young and hard working. In such an achievement, work-oriented society the marginals (sick, elderly, poor, handicapped, and the unborn) are the object of social abuse and disvalue. After all, what can these marginals contribute to the welfare of society? In fact, all they do is make up the welfare rolls which drain our resources. The elderly are on fixed incomes and so their economic buying power is limited. The poor and sick drain resources that could be better used for those who deserve them. The unborn disturb our comfort ethic which sees children as an economic burden and intrusion into the good life. In our urban society children are not viewed as a symbol of hope in the future . . . but as another mouth to feed and an obstacle to realizing our full potential. It is into such a cultural context that the Christian raises her voice and speaks on behalf of those who have no one to plead their cause."

—William Maestri, *Bioethics: A Parish Resource*

4

At Life's End

The marvelous progress of twentieth century medicine has brought great blessings to humanity. Sicknesses that used to be fatal are now curable. Conditions that were once debilitating or crippling are now manageable. More and more men and women live longer than ever before. Yet these achievements have not been an unmixed blessing. Our ability to hold death at bay through ever more ingenious methods often brings us to a point at which we wonder what kind of life we are preserving, and whether the cost in suffering is too high. We have the power to preserve our bodies, but sometimes to the point where they can no longer perform adequately. As a result, increasing numbers of people are facing life-and-death decisions that are sometimes baffling and emotionally draining. Is it ever right to end our own lives or the lives of others in order to spare them further suffering? Must we always do everything possible to keep people alive, or is there a time to yield and let go?

Most of these dramas are played out in hospitals, as families and physicians try to decide what is best for patients who are at death's door. Most, but not all, of these patients are aged; they can be kept alive with respirators and intravenous feeding and a whole array of complex medical machinery. Other stories take place before such points are reached. Increasingly frequent are reported incidents of elderly people committing suicide in order to avoid years of helplessness and dependency. Women and men have confessed to killing their spouses as an act of mercy to spare them further suffering, sometimes voluntarily and sometimes at the sufferer's request. There have been unconfirmed reports of private arrangements whereby patients suffering from debilitating maladies are voluntarily disconnected from life support systems with the support of their families and the cooperation of physicians. Such drastic measures, which would have been unthinkable a few years ago, are being taken in desperation by people who have come to fear life more than death.

The act of mercy killing is called *euthanasia*. It is illegal and immoral. The pressure to change these laws and our way of thinking about euthanasia will probably increase. For medical progress keeps more and more people alive in conditions of acute physical or mental suffering which, in earlier times, would have resulted in death. There is a growing feeling that in the fight against death we are winning the battles but losing the war. Although we can understand and sympathize with those who advocate euthanasia as an act of mercy, our Christian teaching rightly insists that the commandment "Thou shalt not kill" must still be obeyed. For once we convince ourselves that we may put an end to our lives or the lives of others, who knows where it will stop?

There is a real danger that people will not stop at killing to relieve sufferers in extreme cases. Soon the aged, especially the most helpless, will be in danger from those who judge their lives to be "useless." The handicapped may be at special risk. If doctors in great numbers ever let themselves be drawn into these lethal arrangements, they may lose the trust of patients. If hospitals cooperate in putting people to death, the sick may fear to enter them, seeing them not as committed to caring for them but as willing to dispose of them. These are just some of the reasons why there is and should be massive resistance to the very idea of euthanasia.

Passive Euthanasia

There are times when it seems right and necessary to follow a course of action that leads to a patient's death. These decisions at first sight resemble euthanasia but are significantly different. Sometimes called "passive euthanasia," they usually consist in refraining from treatment that would extend the patient's life but are either useless or so burdensome as to be considered inhumane. Let us consider a few of these cases.

An eleven-year-old boy suffering from cystic fibrosis had only a few months to live. For two years he had been in and out of the hospital. He suffered also from bronchial infection, lung abscesses, emphysema, and bronchial pneumonia. The only way to keep him alive was to perform a bronchoscopy, a painful procedure that is only occasionally helpful and which might add at most a few days or weeks to his life. His mother requested that they omit the treatment, keep him as comfortable as possible, and let him die in peace. The hospital staff were reluctant to grant her request since they were accustomed to doing everything they could to preserve and extend life. But the mother was right. It was futile and unintentionally cruel to inflict further painful treatments on the boy when there was no proportional benefit to be gained.

This is the same kind of reasoning we employed earlier in the case of infants with severe birth defects. Painful and dangerous treatments should not be used on patients unless the expected or hoped-for benefit makes it worthwhile. The bronchoscopy would be so painful that it would be pointless to inflict it on the boy, since no significant improvement in his condition was going to be accomplished. The key question must always be: what is best for the patient? In this case, the best service the medical staff could give the boy was to make his last days as comfortable as possible. Medical personnel are rightly trained to do all they can to preserve and lengthen life, but there comes a time when we must accept our limitations and yield to nature.

This is different from active euthanasia. If the doctors grant the mother's request, they are not doing anything to end the boy's life. It is the sickness that is killing him. The doctors and parent have simply chosen *not* to do something. One result of their inaction is that he will probably die a little sooner. But they are not aiming at his death. They have simply decided that a few more days or weeks of pain-wracked life are not enough of a benefit to justify imposing the burden of a useless and painful intervention.

The Use of Respirators

The most common decision of this sort that doctors and families face concerns the use of a respirator. Until a few decades ago, death usually coincided with heart failure. When the heart stopped beating, so did breathing; blood circulation ceased, and death ensued. The respirator, however, breathes for the person and maintains the action of the heart. As a result, some patients who are brain dead or who have lapsed into irreversible comas can be kept "alive" for long periods of time. But what do we mean by "alive" when speaking of someone who can no longer be conscious or interact with other human beings? For the brain dead, such future consciousness is impossible; for the irreversibly comatose, there is no realistic expectation of revival in the foreseeable future.

This was the situation faced by the parents of Karen Ann Quinlan, a young woman who lapsed into a coma after taking drugs and alcohol, and never regained consciousness. She was kept alive for years on a respirator until her family fought and won a long battle in the courts to obtain permission to disconnect the respirator and let her die with dignity. Surprisingly, she continued to live on for ten years afterward, but eventually died. This was a landmark case which significantly changed the course of medical practise. It is now common procedure for physicians and families to discuss beforehand whether to put dying patients on respirators. If the procedure offers no hope of recovery but promises simply to prolong the process of dying, it may be omitted.

Once again we see the difference between this course of action, sometimes called passive euthanasia, and active euthanasia. By refraining from the use of the respirator, or by deciding to discontinue its use, we are not aiming at the death of the patient; this is not a case of mercy killing. True, death may come sooner. But it has been caused by the illness, not by any positive action of the medical staff. If there were any real benefit to be gained by the use of the respirator, it would have been employed. But since it promised only a prolongation of the dying process, it would have been simply a burden for both patient and family. We have already taken every meaningful measure for the patient's welfare; now it is time to let go.

Letting go is never easy. But Christians can look to their faith for help and comfort. Those who follow Jesus Christ believe that he has conquered death by his own death and resurrection and has won for us the promise of eternal life. For Christians, then, physical life is not the highest good we can hope for, nor is physical death the end of all our hopes. We do not deny the sorrow and the pain of loss that comes with death, but we see beyond them and believe that death is the gateway to a fuller life with God.

This faith also helps us to cope with suffering. Jesus won life for us at the price of the excruciating suffering and terrible death of the Cross. By joining our sufferings with his and by opening ourselves to his grace, we are helped to endure pain of both body and spirit and to resist the temptation to take our lives before God calls us.

Removing Food Tubes

If the 1970s were the years of controversy over the use of the respirator, the 1980s were the decade in which experts in medical ethics turned their attention to another form of mechanical life support, the intravenous feeding tube. A group of landmark cases have helped us to deal with the difficult decision of when to use food tubes to preserve the lives of patients who would die without artificial feeding.

Claire Conroy was an 84-year-old nursing home resident who suffered from incurable arteriosclerotic heart disease, diabetes, and hypertension. She could neither speak nor swallow, was severely demented and could only moan or smile in response to some stimuli. Her nephew-guardian requested that her nasogastric food tube be disconnected so that she might be released from a life that had become intolerably and permanently burdensome.

Hilda Peter, 65, suffered a stroke in 1984 and lay in a coma for three years, a condition that doctors said could continue for many years. Her legal guardian requested the removal of the food tube, testifying that Miss Peter had told him repeatedly before lapsing into a coma, "Don't let them keep me alive as a vegetable."

Nancy Ellen Jobes, 31, was four months pregnant when she was in a car accident. She fell into a coma when the doctor removed the fetus, which had died. For six years she remained in an irreversible vegetative state, kept alive by an artificial feeding tube. Her family sued in court for the right to remove it.

Paul Brophy, 49, a comatose firefighter, suffered profound brain damage caused by a burst blood vessel in 1983. His other major organs continued to function, so that he did not need a respirator or other mechanical assistance. But because he could not chew or swallow, he was fed through a surgically implanted tube in his stomach. His wife asked doctors to remove the tube. When the hospital refused on ethical grounds, she went to court seeking legal authority, testifying that he had often said that he would never want to be kept alive "as a vegetable."

In the Conroy case, a judge granted permission to remove the food tube in 1983. While the decision was being appealed, Miss Conroy died. The appeals court nevertheless reversed the judgement as permitting euthanasia. Finally, in 1985, the New Jersey Supreme Court reinstated the original verdict and acknowledged the legal right to refuse such treatment.

The Peter and Jobes cases were also settled by the New Jersey Supreme Court in 1987. The Court permitted the removal of the tubes. It acknowledged that the state has an interest in preserving life, but said those interests weaken—and the individual's right to privacy becomes stronger—"as the degree of bodily invasion increases and the prognosis (for recovering consciousness) dims."

The decision to withhold food from Mr. Brophy was authorized by the Massachusetts Supreme Court in 1986. His death eight days after removal was described by his wife's attorney as "very peaceful."

Courts decide legality, not morality. And not all moralists agree with these decisions. Some feel that removing food tubes is going too far. They agree that turning off a respirator is justifiable when we are eliminating a useless medical procedure. But they see withholding food and water as something quite different—as a deliberate act of refusing basic nourishment. In their view, this amounts to committing active euthanasia. A growing number of moralists and medical experts, on the other hand, consider artificial feeding as a medical treatment, and hence subject to the same norms of judgement as are other medical interventions. If they are useless and provide no hope of recovery, they are simply prolonging the process of dying. And patients who are brain dead or in a persistent vegetative state should be released from bondage to machines. This seems a much more reasonable view, and it seems well on its way to gaining general acceptance.

Who Should Decide?

These hard decisions concerning life's end are sometimes made by patients, sometimes by their families, sometimes by courts of law. In all these cases, doctors and other health care personnel have much to contribute. Ideally, patients themselves should make the hard choices about their own lives. They have the right, and no one can take it away. But sometimes patients are young children or are otherwise incompetent—due either to unconsciousness or senility or other mental handicaps. When that happens, someone has to make the hard choices for them. Who should it be?

Some people would like to leave it to the doctors. This is understandable. Doctors are competent and knowledgeable in an area where people feel incapable of making sound judgements. To them, the doctor is an authority figure. But though they are an indispensable source of information and advice, medical personnel are not necessarily skilled in ethical analysis and decision-making. Family members may not know much about medicine, but they know the patient intimately. They know his or her values and preferences. So they should be the ones to make decisions, once they have availed themselves of the best information and the most expert advice. Doctors can and should help, but the responsibility of deciding is not theirs.

Sometimes the courts have to step in to settle disputes or to protect the rights of patients, but they should not normally be involved in these decisions. They should be the party of last recourse, when patient or family and hospital staffs cannot resolve their differences.

In most court cases the key question is: If the patient could speak, what would he or she want? Testimony is taken concerning the patient's statements of preferences before becoming incompetent. If the patient did not make his or her wishes known in an explicit way, family and close friends are questioned in order to ascertain what the patient presumably would request. The family is expected to know best and to have the patient's welfare at heart. But occasionally their intentions are suspect, and then the court must intervene to make sure that the patient's best interests are served.

The Living Will

None of us wants to put our families through the agonizing dilemmas and trying court actions described above. There is a way to avoid such situations, and it is being used by growing numbers in our society. It is called the Living Will. Through this formal document, we can, while still in good health and in possession of our faculties, let it be clearly known how we want to be treated during life-threatening illnesses. If sickness or accident should deprive us of the ability to communicate with doctors or family, the living will spells out our wishes in detail beforehand. Then doctors and family will have clear directions, and if disagreements end up in court, the judges will be able to hear from us directly through the testament. Here is a sample of what the document might look like. It was published in the *New England Journal of Medicine* in 1976:

Directions for My Care

I want to live a full and long life, but not at all costs. If my death is near and cannot be avoided, and if I have lost the ability to interact with others and have no reasonable chance of regaining this ability, or if my suffering is intense and irreversible, I do not want to have my life prolonged. I would then ask not to be subjected to surgery and resuscitation. Nor would I then wish to have life support from mechanical ventilators, intensive care services, or other life prolonging procedures, including the administration of antibiotics and blood products. I would wish, rather, to have care which gives comfort and support, which facilitates my interaction with others to the extent that this is possible, and which brings peace.

In order to carry out these instructions and to interpret them, I authorize _____ to accept, plan and refuse treatment on my behalf, in cooperation with attending physicians and health personnel. This person knows how I value the experience of living, and how I would weigh incompetence, suffering, and dying. Should it be impossible to reach this person, I authorize _____ to make such choices for me. I have discussed my desires concerning terminal care with them, and I trust their judgement on my behalf.

In addition, I have discussed with them the following specific instructions regarding my care:

(Please continue on back)

Date _____ Signed _____

Witnessed by: 1. _____
               2. _____

Living wills are legally binding in some States but not in others. Even where they do not have the force of law, they are of great help to those who will be caring for us in our last illness. Everyone should give serious thought to drawing up and signing such a document. It can be a very responsible way of dealing with our last days and lifting a heavy burden from those who are closest to us.

Whose Life Is It, Anyway?

The above title appeared in Hollywood and on Broadway several years ago. It is a fictional but realistic case. How would you decide it?

In the play, starring first Tom Conti and then Mary Tyler Moore, and in the movie, starring Richard Dreyfuss, a sculptor emerges from an auto accident paralyzed from the neck down. The paralysis is permanent and irreversible. He is completely alert and rational, can think and feel and talk. But he is totally helpless and confined to a bed in a special unit designed to care for him.

After six months in this condition, after long and calm consideration, he decides that he does not want to live anymore. He realizes that the hospital staff cannot in conscience take his life, so he asks that they simply leave him in a room by himself to die. He knows that such a death will be much more prolonged and painful than one induced by a lethal injection, but it is preferable to the kind of life he is now leading and can look forward to.

The chief of the hospital staff refuses the request as unethical. Some of the staff sympathize with the patient's request. At length he engages a lawyer, and a formal court is convened by a judge in the hospital room. Arguments are heard from both sides—those supporting the patient's request, and those opposing it on the grounds that it involves cooperation in suicide.

Two questions confront us:

1. What decision should the judge render?

2. What do you think of the morality of the patient's request?

5

Love and Sex

After the instinct for survival, the strongest drive we have is for sexual expression. It is a powerful force that opens us up to others and moves us to realize all kinds of possibilities within ourselves—for love, for intimacy, for creating new life. It presents a dark side, too, in that it can bring out the worst in us. It can be used to dominate and manipulate others, to exploit them and make them serve our selfish ends. No other dimension of human beings is at once capable of producing so much goodness and of inflicting so much pain. As women and men we play for high stakes in a game that calls for courage, skill, sensitivity, discipline, and integrity. There are many winners and many losers, and how we fare depends largely on the decisions we make. The moral choices that we make in the matter of sex are among the most difficult we face, and their impact on our lives and the lives of others is often lasting and profound.

Many of these decisions would be hard for us even if we lived in a society in which people pretty much agreed on basic values and standards. But there is so much disagreement among us about sexual ethics, so little consensus even on what sex is all about, that we can often feel confused and alone. Even when we have firm convictions about right and wrong and are clear in our minds about how we ought to act, out instincts are sometimes more powerful than our ideals and can make it seem almost impossible to follow through. Another problem, more obvious when we observe it in others, is our capacity for self-deception. There is no other area of life in which we are more likely to fool ourselves.

Still, it is possible to think clearly and honestly in these matters and to sort out the true and the false. Even though sex is more a matter of the heart than the head, we can and should try to live in a way that is in keeping with our own dignity and with our obligations to others as well as to ourselves. We are, after all, not alone. As Christians we believe that God

has taught us, through Jesus Christ, a good deal about how to love ourselves and one another. As Catholics we have available the guidance of
church leaders who teach in the name of Christ and can give us valuable
assistance in forming our consciences. We also have the community's
shared wisdom which comes to us through competent theologians and
through fellow Christians who try to live in accordance with the Gospels.

Two Extremes

To help us think rightly about the place of sex in our lives, let us consider two extreme positions. The first is the attitude that sex is something
to be ashamed of. This may strike us as so bizarre as to be hardly worth
thinking about. But it does turn up in human history from time to time. Let
us call it *puritanism*. It has gone by other names in earlier centuries, but it
varies very little in the forms it takes. Basically, puritans have negative
feelings about the body. Some of them are religious in a peculiar way.
They value the spiritual side of human nature and look down on the physical. The body and its appetites, especially the sexual, are seen as holding
us back from being spiritual and pure. So the body must be covered up, not
out of normal modesty but out of a sense of shame. Passion is distrusted.
Sensual pleasure must be repressed. Sex is permitted as necessary for marriage and having children, but is not to be enjoyed. For puritans, even the
most wholesome and responsible expressions of our sexuality are likely to
be accompanied by feelings of irrational guilt.

Although puritanism has often been associated with Christianity, it is
completely contrary to the teachings and the spirit of Christ. Our religion
teaches us that God who makes all things good makes us male and female,
blesses the married state, and calls us to increase and multiply and fill the
earth. Moreover, God had made the use of our sexual faculties a source of
intense pleasure in order to encourage us to take on the burdens of married
love and the nurture of children.

At the other extreme, *hedonism* respresents the position of certain ele-
ments in our society who have over-reacted against puritanism.

They see sex as just another appetite, to be satisfied in whatever way
the individual desires. The sexual revolution of the 1960s had a slogan: "If
it feels good, do it." All moral restraints are considered attacks on personal
freedom and privacy. Although its supporters are sometimes accused of
making too much of sex, in reality they tend to trivialize it, robbing it of its

importance as they refuse to recognize any moral limits on behavior. The earlier James Bond novels are typical expressions of this approach; so are the lyrics of the raunchier type of rock music. Of course this is nothing new. In the past there have been other decadent societies which fell into this kind of sexual anarchy.

The truth about sex falls somewhere between the extremes of puritanism and hedonism. The Christian view acknowledges the goodness of sex and accepts it as a gift of God. But we see it as a gift that must be used responsibly, and we recognize that it can often be misused. If we put moral limits on the expression of sex, we do so not out of hatred or fear of the body, but to make sure that our actions are in keeping with Jesus' law of love. We cannot simply obey our instincts. We must express our sexuality in ways that respect the dignity and the rights of all concerned.

Relational Sex

Christians are not the only ones who reject hedonism. Most people recognize the need for some restraint of the sexual appetite. They rightly insist that sexual intimacy must express more than physical desire. They also admit that total intimacy, expressed in intercourse, should in some sense be exclusive; hence promiscuity, or "sleeping around," is disapproved. But they would not say that people should be married before they express their love in sexual intercourse. It is enough that they have what is called a meaningful relationship. That is, they feel genuine affection for each other, but they may not be ready to make any permanent promises to each other or to take full responsibility for each other's lives. They simply agree that as long as their mutual affection lasts they will put no limits on the way they express their affection. In short, as they sometimes put it, "all you need is love."

Although not always stated explicitly in such arrangements, it is understood by both parties that if feelings cool or if more desirable partners appear on the scene, each is free of any obligations to each other. In popular parlance, they "keep their options open." Even the most tender relationships are subject to immediate cancellation. Each person is free to seek the fullest satisfaction of his or her desires.

The reader will recognize this as the kind of sexual morality that operates in the case of roommates or unmarried couples who live together. It also justifies total intimacy between casual lovers, so long as they are not deliberately using each other and they feel that they are expressing genuine love. It is the morality that is taken for granted in most popular entertainment, from soap operas to the most serious movies and stage plays.

For many people who agree with this philosophy, a corollary is that marriage is also subject to cancellation when either husband or wife finds a more attractive lover. Divorce is taken for granted as the obvious solution to this problem. Even extramarital affairs may be approved or at least not condemned. It is usually not called adultery but rather an "affair," and is generally looked upon with tolerance. This is not inconsistent, since the basic principle of relational sex is that people have the right to express the fullest range of their desires, so long as they are attracted to their sexual partners as persons. "Love conquers all." It is also understood, though not always stated, that the only unconditional obligations we have are to ourselves. Not only are we permitted to act this way; we owe it to ourselves.

For those who look to popular entertainment media for their values and standards of conduct, this view of sexual morality is so pervasive and taken-for-granted that it is hard to see any problems with it or to imagine any other norms. There are, however, very serious problems and deficiencies. Let us examine some of them.

First of all, consider the act of sexual intercourse. What is going on here? Two people are naked to each other, totally exposed, completely vulnerable. Their behavior indicates that they are completely open to each other, without reserve. With their body language they are saying, "I belong to you, and you to me. I hold nothing back. I give my *self* to you." But if they have made no promises, no permanent commitment to each other, their hearts and minds are out-of-sync with what their bodies so eloquently proclaim. They are not really giving all without reserve. They are holding back the most important thing of all—themselves. Whether they realize it or not, they are acting out a lie.

This may seem like a very harsh judgment on two people who are simply following some very powerful instincts with no consciously dishonest intentions at all. They themselves will probably resist such judgment with the rationalization that, after all, they are "committed" to each other. But this will not stand up to examination. The dictionary defines commitment as "a pledge or promise to do something." But there is no pledge or promise here; indeed, there is probably a conscious resistance to any sense of obligation. When unpledged lovers say they are "committed," what they really mean is: "I like you a lot, and I wouldn't want you to get hurt. And

I'll be with you as long as I feel this way." Here is an example of what we meant when we said earlier that sex is the area of life in which we are most likely to deceive ourselves and others.

Another weakness of relational sexual morality is the mistaken notion that the closest attachments can be cancelled without damage to either party, so long as both agree beforehand that there will be no binding obligations and either one is free to disengage. The kind of intimacy we have been describing resists such cavalier treatment. We are not talking here of contracts or agreements in which we exchange *things*. We are talking about giving and taking back our very *selves*. Lovers know from painful experience what we are talking about. Rarely do two people who have been this close reach easy mutual agreements to part. What usually happens is that one departs without regret, while the other is left feeling used and betrayed. One party invests more of himself or herself than the other, and on being abandoned suffers loss of self-esteem and perhaps the ability to trust again or to give of oneself without holding back. Indeed, we would probably be worse off if we could avoid being sensitive in this way. We might be spared the pain, but we would lose something more important. If we ever lose the capacity to love unreservedly, to give without strings attached, and to suffer when such love is betrayed, then something will have died in us that makes us truly human.

Finally, relational sex fails to deal responsibly with the question of children. If lovers have no obligations to one another, what about the children they beget through their love? They have several answers, none of them satisfactory. One is to practise artificial birth control. But many do not always take precautions. Even if they do, it is a fact that contraceptives do not always work. It is common today to hear people speak of pregnancy as an "accident." But conception is not an accident; it is the normal consequence of having sexual intercourse! So when contraceptives are not used or fail to work, they may resort to abortion. Or they bear children outside marriage, these children, in turn, being deprived of a father's presence and support. Then the casualities of uncommitted sex are not only the lovers who fail each other, but also innocent bystanders in the persons of children who are unwanted or neglected or simply eliminated. This is a dimension of uncommitted sex that people persist in ignoring, but which simply will not go away.

A Christian Approach

As Catholics and other Christians see it, God made us male and female so that we could love one another in a special way. Men and women are invited to share their bodies and indeed their whole lives in bringing new life into the world. The sexual side of us reaches fulfillment in a relationship that is not only meaningful but also exclusive and permanent. This is how women and men achieve their possibilities as lovers—as husbands and wives, mothers and fathers.

This vision includes romantic love but goes much further. It says that if people want to be intimate, they must care for each other. If they want to be totally intimate, then they should be totally committed to each other, holding nothing back, taking full responsibility for each other. This is why sexual intercourse is restricted to those who are married to each other.

When a man and a woman relate to each other this way, they are ready to marry—to make a home, a family, a life together. This is what real love is all about. It is serious but joyful. It calls for unselfishness and sacrifice, but opens up tremendous possibilities. It achieves the union not only of bodies but also of hearts and minds.

This view of sex is based on Christ's law of love. We have obligations not only to ourselves but to one another. Commitment means what it says: for richer or poorer, for better or worse, in sickness and in health, till death parts us. If men and women are not ready to make such promises, then they should not say with their bodies what they do not really mean. Otherwise they risk doing harm to themselves, to each other, and to their children. This is why premarital and extramarital sex and adultery are forbidden.

The Christian tradition does not say 'no' to sex, but sometimes it says 'Not yet, not until we mean what we say.' Not until love is more than a passing episode. This is a high ideal that makes serious demands and calls for unselfishness and a willingness to make sacrifices. Many of us feel unable to measure up to such an ideal, and we are right. Without God's help we could not do it. But that help is promised to us by Christ himself.

Homosexuality

Until now, we have been speaking as if everyone were heterosexual. But of course this is not the case. It is estimated that four to ten percent of the population is homosexual in orientation. What are the hard choices that face this significant and troubled minority?

Why some people are attracted to their own sex and not to the other remains a mystery. We have overcome some of our ignorance about this condition, but complete understanding still eludes us. Are homosexuals born that way, or do they become so through early experiences or environment? The debate goes on but is not much help to the homosexual person. Is it possible to change this orientation? For some, yes. Psychotherapy has helped some of those who seek treatment. But most are unable to alter their condition and must come to terms with it. How is this to be done?

The first thing to understand is that there is no moral fault in *being* homosexual. People do not choose this condition; they only become aware of it as they grow up, and by then it is too late for most of them to do anything about it. The Catholic Church's teaching is clear and strong on this point. Homosexuals are not to be rejected or condemned for being the way they are. Christians are commanded to love them just as they love anyone else. Mockery and harassment or discrimination against them is a sin. So how should we treat homosexuals? Like anyone else. They are our neighbors, and we are to love them as we love ourselves.

On the other hand, we must admit that homosexuality is not just another sexual orientation, simply different from heterosexuality but just as good. In an understandable but misguided attempt to assert their dignity and their right to respect and fair treatment, some gays and their supporters try to treat it as simply an alternative lifestyle. It is not. Our religious tradition, beginning with the book of Genesis in the Bible, clearly teaches that male and female are meant to complement each other. The sexual appetite is directed not only to the expression of love but also to the begetting of children. Since homosexuals are unable to express their sexuality in a way that is open to the transmission of life, intimate physical union with a person of the same sex is fundamentally out of order. This is not to say that they are evil in any way, but simply that they are unable to engage in the genital expression of sexuality in the normal way. Hence the Church teaches that homosexual activity in the form of genital expression is wrong.

This is a very difficult truth for many homosexual persons and some of their advocates to accept. Some reject it because they are moral relativists who deny that there is any objective right or wrong in the matter. Others have more serious objections that command our earnest and compassionate consideration. They point out that all human beings have a need to be loved and to experience some kind of intimacy. Are homosexuals to be denied this basic human need because of a condition which is not their fault and over which they have no control?

Arguments like these are not to be casually dismissed. They constitute a real cry of pain that deserves our sympathy and respect. But the fact remains that to seek intimacy in this way is disordered and doomed to frustration. It may help to remember that homosexuals are not the only ones who are required to forgo genital-sexual expression. There are men and women who have taken religious vows of celibacy as brothers, priests, and sisters. There are lay women and men who have chosen the single state of life. And there are those who may marry in the future but are at present single. All of these are required to live up to Christian norms of sexual conduct, including the prohibition of intercourse for those who are not married. Nor do these people live lives devoid of love. They integrate their sexuality into lives of generosity and service. They achieve intimacy on many levels. Homosexuals can, with God's grace and the help of prayer and self-discipline, live full lives as well.

Many say that the sexual morality presented here is too idealistic. They feel that ordinary people cannot live up to such high standards of conduct. They doubt that our instincts can be controlled when such powerful drives are involved. But what are the alternatives? They have been tried and found wanting. "Free sex" in all its forms has been a disaster. The relational sex compromise has not been much better. Together they have brought us disease, a multibillion dollar sex industry that exploits and corrupts, broken families, social breakdown, and over a million abortions a year. The sexual revolution has been won at the price of far too much human destruction.

There is no easy, problem-free way to a happy sex life. Being an honest, caring, sensitive lover is an achievement that demands the best of us. The best things in life are *not* free. But they are worth the struggle. The Christian ideal is still the most successful way that we have found to make us great lovers and thus enrich our lives and those of the men and women we meet on our way.

Marriage in the Church

"As much as they might like to, no couple can rewrite the meaning of sexual intercourse. It is tied to committed love; it is tied to life-giving. When a person engages in sexual intercourse it is a sign of giving one's very self, whether one intends to or not. To let my actions be a sign of self-gift if my heart knows the truth to be different is to lie.

"We must pledge ourselves to be true to what is really happening. Is our love so real that it is truly permanent, exclusively centered on this one person with whom I wish to link my life forever, the kind of love which could some day bring forth children as its sign? Then we are ready not for 'second best' but for the joy of marriage in Christ—not in any sense 'a piece of paper from the Church,' but a chance to stand at the altar before God and fellowman and say 'We love one another and want our love to last forever. We ask you to respect this, to rejoice with us, to help us keep it so.' This is marriage in the Church."

—Francis J. Mugavero, Bishop of Brooklyn

6

When Children Are A Problem: Birth Control

Usually the birth of a baby brings great joy and is called a "blessed event." But in our times, perhaps more than ever in human history, the bringing of children to birth is viewed with anxiety and fear. Unlike the generations before us, great numbers of women and men want to avoid conception and birth. They resort to birth control to avoid conceiving and, when this fails, to abortion. This has raised painful and divisive moral questions both within the church and in society as a whole. Before we address these questions, let us see why children have come to be seen as a burden rather than a blessing.

Until the twentieth century, the vast majority of married couples lived in conditions which made large families desirable. Besides the usual reasons that make children wanted, there was the fact that they were of great economic advantage. They went to school for only a few years. On the farm they soon contributed significant labor. Even when most families moved into cities, the children had earning power at a young age, thanks to the need for unskilled labor and the absence of child labor laws. So, for the most part, the more children you had the better off you were. And since children's diseases killed so many, it might take several pregnancies even to raise a family of moderate size.

By the 1920's, however, several factors created problems, especially in industrialized countries. Medical progress made childbearing safer and reduced the incidence of infant and childhood mortality. Industrial progress and the enactment of child labor reform legislation, as well as the need for longer and longer periods of schooling, made children no longer economic assets but rather an increasing financial burden. Raising large numbers of children and paying for increasingly costly education became a load that fewer and fewer families felt able to afford. Thus, toward the end of the second decade of this century, birth control for the first time became a real issue for large numbers of people.

Religious people turned to their churches for guidance in this matter. All the churches did not give the same advice, but Roman Catholic Church teaching was clearly against artificial birth control, for reasons which we will explain shortly.

The sexual revolution in the 1950's and 1960's increased the pressure to refrain from having children. As society became increasingly tolerant of sex outside of marriage, more and more couples found themselves in situations where children were undesirable. These were premarital and extramaritial relationships which lacked the stability of marital unions. People in such arrangements usually do not want the responsibility of caring for children. When contraception was not used or did not work, they did not want to bring unborn children to term. So pressure was brought to legalize abortion, and in the 1970's the United States and several other countries yielded to the demand. Thus, abortion has become, for many, a fallback method of birth control. Married couples who feel unable or unwilling to care for the children they conceive have also resorted to abortion in increasing numbers. And adolescents, for whom premarital sex has become more and more common, have also come to look upon abortion as the solution to unwanted pregnancies. The most common public response to this practise has been to urge teenagers to use contraceptives instead, but with conspicuous lack of success.

The Catholic Church, together with many other religious communities, has condemned abortion as a much greater evil than contraception, for reasons to be explained in the next chapter. But this brief historical survey helps us to understand how we have arrived at the present state of affairs, where so many men and women feel so strongly that they must keep separate the expression of love and the bearing of children.

Birth Control

The first thing that needs to be said about birth control is that, in one sense, everyone is in favor of it, including the Roman Catholic church. Common sense as well as religious tradition tell us that we should only have as many children as we can properly take care of. This, of course, means different things to different people. For some, large families work out just fine; parents find great joy in raising several children, and the children themselves enrich one another's lives. For others, smaller households are the more prudent course, for reasons of health or energy or economic necessity. There is no one standard for all. At any rate, the church has never taught that couples should simply have as many children as they can. As we pointed out above, in previous centuries that was just what most people did, because in the social and economic conditions of those times it made sense. But now that the upbringing of children is so much more demanding, we are encouraged to keep families at a manageable size, so that each child can receive the attention and education he or she deserves. And for some couples that will imply some form of birth control.

The question is, what kind of birth control? There is a *natural* way of limiting or spacing births, paying heed to cycles of fertility and taking care to limit lovemaking from time to time to those periods when conception is not likely to take place. There is also an *artificial* way to exercise birth control, using various forms of contraceptives to frustrate the natural consequences of sexual intercourse. It is this artificial mode of birth control, called *contraception*, that has been condemned by official church teaching.

This teaching is very puzzling to many people today, who cannot imagine why it should make any difference how people express their love in marriage. Before we try to explain the reasons for this prohibition, we should understand why many find it incomprehensible. Remember the relativists and pragmatists we met in earlier chapters? For the relativists, there is no right or wrong until we think about it. Each person must decide what seems best for herself or himself. And they usually decide on pragmatic grounds, asking only: Does it work? If a small family or no family is what the couple desires, the only decision is to find the most efficient way to prevent conception. (Actually, the only foolproof method is abstinence; but, for reasons not too hard to figure out, this way is rejected beforehand.) No other questions need to be asked.

Christians look at birth control from a very different point of view. For those who follow Christ and try to live by his values, married love and children are gifts of God that are meant to go together. We can see this when we look at the way God made us male and female and invited us to be united in love. When we express this love through sexual intercourse, a frequent result is the conception of children. This life-giving dimension is built into the very nature of married love because God meant it to be so. So when husbands and wives give themselves to each other in a way that is open to new life, they are cooperating with God in a wonderful way to bring forth sons and daughters made in the divine image and destined to share in the fullness of God's own life. By the same token, when they take artificial measures to frustrate the life-giving possibilities of married love, they fail to live up to the ideal that God has clearly marked out for them.

We are, of course, speaking here only of the love that is expressed in marriage. Unmarried lovers have many good reasons for trying to avoid having children, but they should not be having sexual relations in the first place. It is only in the context of a stable home that children should be brought into the world. That is one of the reasons why full sexual expression is restricted to those who have taken full responsibility for each other and their children in the sacred pledge of matrimony.

Difficulties Remain

Even when husbands and wives understand and accept this teaching, they may experience great difficulty in trying to live up to it. Some or all of the problems described above that face parents today may leave them feeling unable to pursue this ideal, no matter how attractive it may be. As they struggle to resolve this conflict in a responsible way, they are aware that Catholics are deeply divided in their response to this teaching on birth control. Our treatment of the issue would not be complete if we did not recognize these divisions and try to make some sense of them. Let us examine these disagreements in some detail, find out what is at the root of them, and try to draw some practical conclusions for guidance in the formation of conscience.

Nearly all Catholics accept the ideal of marriage as life-giving as well as love-giving. They agree that children are a normal part of any Christian marriage in the sense that spouses should be willing to have the children that God sends them. When engaged couples are interviewed before contracting marriage in church, they are required to affirm before God that they are willing to accept children as the fruit of their love. Most would agree that contraception at least falls short of that ideal. But suppose we put the question this way: is it ever right to go against the ideal? To the rule that spouses should not use contraceptives, are there any exceptions? Here is where Catholics disagree.

The Popes who have written on this subject have consistently stated that there are no exceptions to the rule against contraceptives. While expressing sympathy and compassion for couples who find it difficult to do so, they say the obligation nevertheless remains to leave every expression of married love open to the possibility of new life. Many other church leaders, theologians, and other lay people accept this teaching and encourage one another to follow it as well. Some of these do not see how they could do otherwise and still call themselves loyal and obedient members of the church.

On the other hand, large numbers of Catholics, including respected theologians and others, both lay and clerical, respectfully disagree. While holding to the ideal of fruitful married love and rejecting contraception as the normal practise, they insist that there may be times when its use is justified. Such a decision, they warn, is not to be made lightly but only after careful and prayerful deliberation. But if spouses conclude that this is the only way to serve their marriage, their family, and the community, they may rightly act in accordance with their deepest personal convictions.

Living with the Pain

Divisions like these among Catholics are a source of pain to everyone. While we are used to disputes with our fellow citizens about religious and moral matters and manage to live in harmony despite our disagreements, it is not so easy to do so when the arguments are with members of our own church. Nevertheless, it looks as though some of these disagreements are going to be with us for a long time, and we must find a way to live with them and still be one in Christ. This does not mean that we should deny the disputes or make believe they do not matter. Strong families do not deal with conflict that way. Instead they speak honestly and do not paper over their differences. But they do so in a spirit of love and respect. To this end, it may be helpful to see how those with whom we disagree arrive at their positions. This does not solve all problems or immediately resolve all conflicts, but it can contribute to better understanding.

What is often taking place here is two groups of people doing moral theology in different ways and hence arriving at different conclusions. Those who argue against any exceptions to the rule forbidding contraception usually concentrate on the *individual acts of love within marriage,* while those who admit exceptions tend to focus on the *marriage as a whole.*

The first group begins with the principle that sex within marriage should be life-giving as well as love-giving, and that God has made this perfectly clear to us. They therefore conclude that the individual expressions of love which are part of that marriage must not prevent the possibility of new life. Hence any use of contraceptives is, by their very nature, forbidden. There can be no exceptions.

The second group also starts with the principle that sex within marriage should be life-giving as well as love-giving. But instead of applying it to the individual acts of love in isolation, they apply it to the marriage itself, i.e., to the whole of their life together. They ask: is this *marriage* open to life? Thus, for example, a couple may have four children; today this is generally considered a fairly large family. But for economic or for other serious reasons they have occasionally used artificial birth control for limited times in order to space the births over a longer period. To this way of thinking, the occasional use of contraceptives, while not ideal, is not what matters most. What does matter is that their lived relationship, their marriage as a whole, has been fruitful. The spirit rather than the letter of the law has been obeyed. The Lord's command to "increase and multiply" has been fulfilled.

These are two very different ways of thinking, and it is not surprising that they yield different conclusions. But both groups are trying seriously to find God's will and to preserve the basic values of Christian marriage. They are not as far apart as they may seem.

What does all this have to do with the way individual couples, husbands and wives, make the hard choices about when and how to have children?

Like many of your fellow Catholics, you may feel uncomfortable with the idea of any use of artificial birth control. Perhaps the way of thinking that focuses on the morality of individual acts makes more sense to you. Maybe even more important to you is the sense of security that comes with knowing that you are acting in full accord with official church teaching. These are very good reasons for seeking other ways of regulating the size of your family if reasons of health or economics or other important considerations indicate that this is advisable. You may decide to use periodic continence or "rhythm," confining sexual relations to those times of the month when conception is not likely to occur. If the wife's cycle is irregular or difficult to estimate, then the method known as natural family planning may be employed. When properly understood and used, it is an accurate way of knowing whether she is fertile or not at a given time. It is natural, safe, and more reliable than contraceptive methods.

If these considerations are not convincing for you, and if you and your spouse are convinced that these methods will not work for you, you may feel it necessary to employ some artificial means of birth control. If you do, make sure that your choice is not a selfish one. Seek advice from someone you respect and trust, and take the matter to prayer. Ask for God's help, even as you take responsibility for your life together. Keep attentive to God's voice and listen for it not only in your own heart but in the life of the church. These are hard choices, and we can sometimes feel lonely in making them. But we are never alone.

7

When Children Are A Problem: Abortion

A pregnant woman in Washington, D.C., pleaded guilty to a charge of forging $700 in checks. Since it was her first offense, she would normally have been given probation. But when tests revealed that she had used cocaine, the judge sent her to jail until the baby was due in order to protect it from drug abuse. While some people applauded his action, others criticized him for creating rights for the fetus that have no foundation in law.

Another pregnant woman in Long Island was charged with child neglect because she used cocaine and failed to obtain prenatal care. The judge admitted that according to law she had an absolute right to have an abortion. But since she had decided to have the baby, he ruled that there is no reason to treat a child in the womb any differently from a child outside the womb. In a similar case, another judge took an opposing view, saying that the state had no authority to regulate women's bodies simply because they are pregnant.

A lawyer, commenting on these and similar cases, remarked how ironic it was that at a time when the state was being criticized for not intervening in cases of severe child abuse, it was also being criticized for intervening to protect children before birth. She pointed out that these cases involved a balancing of the mother's rights against the rights of the child, and that sometimes the two are in conflict.

These are just a few of the numerous real life stories that point up the conflicting and sometimes self-contradictory attitudes that Americans have concerning children. Nothing divides our country more sharply than the abortion issue. Positions on both sides of the question have hardened since the Supreme Court declared anti-abortion laws unconstitutional in 1973. On one side are citizens trying to protect unborn children's most basic right, the right to life. On the other are citizens just as determined to protect the rights of privacy and freedom of choice. They are like two nations speaking completely different languages.

In the previous chapter we reviewed the historical developments that have made child-bearing problematic for so many in our society. When birth control is neglected or fails to work, abortion is seen as the solution to unwanted pregnancies. The first thing we notice is that a great variety of reasons are given for seeking an abortion, ranging from the very serious to the very trivial. At one end of the scale we have the victims of rape and incest and those for whom a pregnancy presents a threat to life. At the other end we have people whose vacation schedules would be disrupted or who have learned through prenatal diagnosis that the baby is of the wrong sex. In between are a host of more or less serious concerns, including economic hardship, teenage pregnancy, and prenatal diagnosis of birth defects.

There are three general positions taken in response. One says that no matter what the reasons are, the life of the unborn child takes precedence over all other considerations. A second says that abortion is justified only by the most serious concerns. A third says that any reason is good enough, since all that matters is the woman's right to privacy and freedom of choice. Those who hold some form of the second position are trying for a more moderate approach than the other two. They often add a further consideration, the age of the fetus. For them, less serious grounds are required during the first trimester of pregnancy than in the second or third.

The Catholic church, together with other religious bodies and with some people of no specific religious allegiance, teaches that the unborn child has the right to life. This is not a religious doctrine strictly speaking, but a moral judgement that anyone of any church or no church should be able to make. Once a child is conceived, a process has begun which will normally result in a fully human being. It must be treated in accordance with Jesus' law of love which calls upon us to do no harm to one another. Whether the child is wanted by its parents or not, it has the right to be treated in accordance with its dignity as an emerging human person. This dignity is bestowed not by the parents or by the state but by God its creator. Any human law which permits the child to be killed simply because the parents will it is an unjust law, because it claims to give a right which does not exist.

This right to life of the unborn child was almost universally acknowledged for centuries. Doctors and nurses have always witnessed to it when they took the Hippocratic oath and swore not to participate in abortions. It is only in the last years of the twentieth century that this pledge has been abandoned by members of the medical profession. What arguments have been offered to justify a practise which was condemned by civilized peoples for centuries?

The arguments of those who promote abortion can be roughly divided into two classes. The first look at the reality of abortion and contend that it is really not so bad. The second say that it doesn't really matter, as long as it expresses a free choice.

Arguments for Abortion

Let's look first at the reasons offered why abortion is really not so bad, and see why they do not stand up to serious examination. *The fetus is not really human.* It is strange that this rationalization is being offered at a time when science is telling us more about life in the womb than we ever knew before. The more we learn about prenatal life, the more we are struck by the extraordinary development and the range of experiences available to the unborn child. Within three weeks there is a heartbeat and the beginning of a nervous system. A two-month old fetus sucks a thumb, sleeps and wakes up, makes a fist. At 18 weeks the mother can feel the baby kicking and punching.

The fetus is not yet a person. Those who argue this way say that we are not yet persons until we have achieved consciousness and self-awareness. But this is a very arbitrary way of deciding when a human being becomes a person. When opponents of this view pointed out that newborn infants lack this self-awareness, and that the argument could logically be used to justify infanticide, its defenders did not even blink. They admitted the conclusion and made a case for eliminating infants with severe birth defects. Remember Infant Doe in Bloomington? Once you start the killing, it's hard to know where to stop. Who's next?

Abortion is better than bringing unwanted children into the world. But unwanted by whom? There are more couples trying to adopt babies than there are babies available. And even if this weren't so, what are we talking about? Disposable items? Disposable people? Is there a difference? If parents refuse or are unable to nurture and protect their children, society must step in. We are all responsible for one another. We already recognize this in establishing social service agencies which arrange for the care of children who are victims of poverty or neglect or abuse.

Legalized abortions are safer than illegal abortions. They may be safer, but does that make them right? What this argument really shows is that women who are desperate enough to seek abortions need more help than society is willing to give. There are many church-related and other private institutions dedicated to helping women deal with unwanted pregnancies in responsible and caring ways. Legalized abortion is simply a way to ignore problems—and problem people—by sweeping them out of sight and out of existence.

What a woman does with her body is her own business. This is true. But if she is pregnant, there is now someone else's body involved—her child's. The fetus is not just a piece of tissue. It is a living, breathing human being on the way to birth and its own independent existence. How should we treat this other person's body?

The fetus has no existence of its own; it is completely dependent on its mother. The fetus does have an existence of its own. It has its own nervous system, its own bloodstream, its own genetic makeup, all distinct from the mother's. True, it is dependent on its mother. But does dependence deprive people of their rights and make them disposable? Do we devalue newborn babies and small children because they are helpless? What do arguments like these say about the people who make them? And if we accept arguments like these, what does it say about us as a society?

Arguments for Free Choice

Perhaps because these arguments for abortion are so threadbare, or maybe because they are not very convincing even to those who make them, they are not used as much as they used to be in the great national debate on this issue. Instead, what we increasingly hear is an argument that has been reduced to a slogan. It says, simply, that people should have a choice. Instead of calling themselves "pro-abortion," they now call themselves "pro-choice." This clever slogan has much to recommend it. Besides fitting easily on demonstration placards, it is easy to understand, requires no logical thinking, and appeals to values that are very dear to Americans: freedom and self-determination. Who wants to be against freedom? Who wants to deprive people of the power to choose?

Of course people are free to choose. Every human person is endowed with free will. But *how* should we choose? And are our choices always good ones? All of us know from painful personal experience that from time to time we have made bad choices. We have hurt others, violated their rights, failed to care for those who had a call on our concern. In traditional religious terms, this is just another way of saying we are all sinners. "Sin" is a term somewhat out of fashion today. But even nonreligious people admit that they are capable of doing wrong. That is part of being free.

So when pro-abortion people say they want to be free to choose, our answer is simple. You *are* free. But to choose *what*? And *how* will you decide? If you decide to have an abortion, you are exercising your freedom. But what are you *doing*? What they really mean, of course, is that they want the *legal* right to choose. They are afraid that laws may be passed limiting access to abortion. In the minds of many, legality is the same as morality. Anything goes, so long as "there's no law against it." But, as we pointed out earlier, there is a big difference between legality and morality. Slavery was once legal in parts of this country. In those States, people got used to seeing human beings bought and sold like cattle. They figured it must be alright, since a great many people did it and there was no law against it. Indeed, some churches even tried to find justification for it in the Bible! But more and more people came to see that it was profoundly immoral, and eventually the slaves were set free. Even so, we were still stuck with racial segregation laws right up to 1963. After the tremendous struggles of the civil rights movement, the United States finally decided that what had been taken for granted for a hundred years was morally despicable, and, as a result, passed a national civil rights act outlawing racial segregation. (South Africa is still working on this.) As another example, women were denied the right to vote until 1920, when the 19th Amendment to the Constitution put an end to a great injustice that had been done to half our people for more than a century.

The denial of freedom to slaves, or of equal opportunity to blacks, did not become morally wrong the day they became illegal. The denial of voting rights to women did not become unjust the day the Constitution was amended in their favor. Those denials were always wrong. It just took time for the law to catch up with people's sense of fairness and justice. So also with abortion. The fact that it is legal gives us no guarantee that it is worthy of us as human beings. So when we are faced with hard choices, as in the abortion question, we must look beyond legal statutes in order to form our conscience.

Hand-in-hand with the pro-choice mentality goes a strategy for dealing with opponents of abortion. They complain that people in the pro-life movement are trying to impose their morality on those who disagree with them. Here we recognize our old friend, moral relativism, which says that nothing is right or wrong in itself and that morality is all in the eye of beholder. So no one can tell anyone else that they are doing right or wrong. That would be imposing their morality, insisting that people agree with them in a matter not of truth but of taste.

As we pointed out earlier, this is simply absurd. Every day we impose our morality on our fellow citizens. When we catch them stealing or mugging or polluting the environment, we fine them and put them in prison. When the judge sentences them, he speaks for society and says, in effect, that they have abused their freedom. They have made choices that violated the property, the persons, and the lives of their victims. And let us be clear about this. Robbery and murder are not wrong because we have laws against them. It's the other way around. We have laws against robbery and murder because they are wrong. We are never going to get a handle on this whole tragic issue or abortion until we get beyond talking about legality and learn how to talk about morality. Even passing laws against abortion will not solve the problem, unless we educate people's hearts and minds and make them sensitive once again to the sacredness of life and the dignity of all human beings, even the helpless and the weak.

Are There Exceptions?

Even people who agree with what we have said so far sometimes have second thoughts. Even when you agree that abortion is a great evil, are there some times when it seems better than going through with a pregnancy? Granted, some of the reasons why women seek abortions are less serious and even trivial, but surely not all. We can all think of cases, both real and imagined, when bearing a child is a terrible burden. Are there any exceptions?

What makes it difficult to allow exceptions, even when the mother's plight evokes all our sympathy, is the fact that we are weighing even the most severe hardship against the life of the child. What can you compare to the value of a human life?

One thing comparable is the mother's life. If a pregnancy threatens the life or health of the mother, she should abort. Fortunately, thanks to progress in medical science, such instances are becoming more and more rare. Surveys indicate that less than one per cent of abortions in America involve a threat to the woman's health.

What about the cases in which pregnancy has occurred because of rape or incest? Here are instances when all our instincts tell us that a woman should not have to bear a child under such conditions. Is there any way that we can justify abortion and spare her further anguish?

For an answer, we can examine in detail the first seven to nine days in the life of the fertilized ovum, before it is implanted in the uterus. During this period it is called a zygote, and it displays some significant characteristics. First of all, it is conservatively estimated that at least fifty per cent of all fertilized ova are never implanted; they are spontaneously wasted. Secondly, if twinning is going to take place, it will take place during this pre-implantation period. Thirdly, if untwinning is to occur, it is likewise during this time. These last two phenomena raise some interesting questions. What are we to say is happening here? Is one human being becoming two? Are two human beings becoming one? This seems absurd.

It seems reasonable to infer from these data that at this stage of pregnancy we are not dealing with a human being in the full sense of the word. Certainly it is not yet possessed of stable individuality. Therefore it does not merit the same degree of protection that we grant to an established pregnancy. This is not to say that zygotes are of no value and may be disposed of for any reason at all. By no means! It is still part of the process of becoming a human person. But in the agonizing cases of rape and incest, when we balance the suffering of the woman against the rather tenuous hold that the zygote has on individuality, a good case can be made for evacuation procedures during that first week. After that time, with the pregnancy fully established, it is hard to justify such measures.

If a woman comes to a doctor to get an abortion, he will reassure her: "No problem; we can terminate it right here." If another woman comes to him for a regular pregnancy check-up, he will tell her: "Your baby is doing fine." More than language is being corrupted here. We are, as a people, getting used to killing our children. The courts, the news and entertainment media, and prominent figures like television and movie stars are united in a vast campaign against the rights of the unborn. Our young people grow up taking it for granted, uncritically swallowing the slogans and rationalizations that pass for honest discourse. We live in the midst of a great evil. If we object to the slaughter, we are made to feel like reactionary bigots.

In a world gone mad, those who are sane can often feel helpless and alone. But we must not lose heart. Most people who crusade for abortion or mindlessly accept it are not evil or consciously hypocritical. They are mostly weak and confused, caught up in a corrupt system that is so pervasive that they cannot imagine any other possibilities. Meanwhile we who know what is really happening can keep our minds clear and call things by their right name. The rest is up to God.

Birth Is Only the Beginning

"Our moral, political, and economic responsibilities do not stop at the moment of birth. Those who defend the right to life of the weakest among us, must be equally visible in support of the quality of life of the powerless among us: the old and the young, the hungry and the homeless, the undocumented immigrant and the unemployed worker. Such a quality of life posture translates into specific political and economic positions on tax policy, employment generation, welfare policy, nutrition and feeding programs, and health care. Consistency means we cannot have it both ways: We cannot urge a compassionate society and vigorous public policy to protect the rights of the unborn and then argue that compassion and significant public programs on behalf of the needy undermine the moral fiber of the society or are beyond the proper scope of governmental responsibility."

—Joseph Cardinal Bernardin, Archbishop of Chicago

In Defense of the Unborn

The following joint statement was issued on April 21, 1989, in defense of those who participated in Operation Rescue, an organized popular movement aimed at blocking access to abortion facilities in various cities in the United States:

The Catholic Bishops of the State of New Jersey express their solidarity with all those who choose to defend the rights of the unborn, including those who participate in public demonstrations. We reject the extraordinary punitive actions being taken against members of Operation Rescue and call on all members of our society to join in this rejection. We esteem the courage of those who have chosen jail as a means of bringing the plight of the unborn to everyone's attention. We reject violence as an instrument in the pursuit of any goal, however worthy. We also deplore the harsh sentences imposed by courts that tend to inhibit the exercise of Constitutional guarantees of freedom of religion, the right of free speech and the right of free association.

We recall in the not too distant past the effective demonstration and sit-ins protesting the denial of civil rights to black citizens of our country. They helped to reduce injustice and bigotry. Surely the killing of an unborn child is the ultimate denial of basic human and civil rights . . . .

The Bishops of New Jersey join with all those fighting for the rights of the unborn.

We call on every citizen and every legislator to join in protecting the rights of the unborn and the rights of those with the courage to speak against the destruction of human life.

As a State and a Nation we have the tradition of being life-giving people. We have the resources to offer alternatives to destruction of life. We must find a place in our minds, hearts and homes for the unborn. We must also protect the rights of those decrying destruction of the unborn.

We pray that God will continue to give strength and courage to those who testify to the sanctity of all human life. We thank God that there are people willing to sacrifice themselves for the innocent, unborn children.

8

War and Peace

When we look at the hard choices we have examined up to now, we see a great variety of moral questions facing us today. We have talked about how children should be brought into the world, and how to care for the unborn and for those born with serious handicaps. At the other end of life, we asked ourselves how far we should use our marvelous powers of medicine and medical technology to sustain life in the terminally ill. We examined each of them in the light of Jesus' law of love and tried to find out how he would want us to treat our sisters and brothers in these difficult situations.

Although the issues covered a wide range of life's problems and were very different from one another, they did have three features in common. First, they were all, in one way or another, matters of life and death. Second, they were for the most part problems that we must face as individuals: If I believe in God and really wish to follow Jesus Christ, what should I do? Third, they concerned our treatment of the weak, the helpless, the handicapped; those who depend on others and whose lives are sometimes seen as unproductive and expendable.

There are other life-and-death questions that we must deal with, not just as individuals but together as members of society. They concern not the weak and the helpless but those who threaten our lives and property. Some of these enemies come from outside, and in trying to defend ourselves we have to make choices concerning war and peace. In a world that lives under the shadow of the arms race and the threat of war, how should we go about ensuring the safety of our people? In the face of international terrorism and recurring crises that threaten the peace of the world, how should we as a nation respond? How can we best contribute to justice and peace?

War and Peace

The decision to wage war has always been the most anguished that a nation must make. Whether the action is forced on us by an enemy attack or is a conscious choice among alternatives, it has involved death and destruction to thousands and even millions. And this is true even of conventional wars. But since the dawning of the atomic age in 1945 and the development of nuclear weapons shortly thereafter, the stakes have become so high that we can barely comprehend them. The threat of nuclear war is a threat not just to millions or even to whole peoples, but to the very earth itself. Our world, as we know it, could cease to exist if there were ever a full-scale nuclear exchange. This prospect is so overwhelming that we do not even want to think about it. We naturally shrink from thinking about ourselves as living on the brink of worldwide destruction. So most of the time we go about the affairs of our daily lives as if all were normal, as if the missiles were not in place on hair-trigger alert. Of course we know they are there, and that a miscalculation or an accident could send them on their deadly way. But we try to keep the realization deep in the back of our minds so that we can get on with business as usual.

But from time to time these unpleasant realities force their way into our consciousness so that we have to think about them whether we want to or not. An international incident may happen: a plane or ship is hit by accident or design, and the armed forces go on alert. A proposal is made by one side or another to reduce the number of nuclear weapons, and the people's leaders and their representatives must frame a reply. Periodic thaws in superpower relations raise the hopes of some for peace, but arouse deep suspicions in others. Fear and distrust keep rival nations armed to the teeth, each reluctant to let down its guard. Through all these shifting tides, the arms race seems to have a life of its own, expanding the arsenals of destruction to ever higher levels.

Many people are deeply convinced that it is wrong not only to use these weapons but even to have them. Some of them publicly oppose our country's production and maintenance of nuclear arms, demonstrating and disrupting and even going to jail to demonstrate their concern. On the other side are vast numbers who are just as convinced that these weapons must be maintained in order to keep the peace. They believe that some of our enemies understand no language but force and the threat to use force. And rival nations think the same of us. The resulting stalemate not only makes the world a series of armed camps but also drains money and other resources that nations need to properly feed and clothe and house their people. It is a fearsome and frustrating state of affairs that keeps us all in danger and drains the energies needed for real human development.

Nuclear war and the threat of nuclear war through the arms race are not the only issues, either. In the almost half a century since the first atomic bombs fell, there have been no nuclear conflicts but several conventional wars. In some of these the United States has been deeply involved. We always hope that each conventional war will be our last, but the possibility remains that we may go to war again.

What is a Christian to say about all this? Does our faith offer us any guidance? What would Jesus say? What should we, who call ourselves his followers, think and do about the arms race? About the threat of nuclear war? About taking part in conventional wars? Is our religion of any use to us when we face the hard questions of war and peace?

A good way to begin to answer these questions is to consider three ways of thinking about the morality of war. They are *militarism, pacifism*, and *just war theory*.

Militarism

Militarism is a completely pragmatic approach to war. To the militarist, the only question to ask before going to war is, can we win? And once involved in war, the only measure of right and wrong is, does it contribute to victory or defeat? As the old coach said about football, winning isn't everything, it's the *only* thing. War has its own rules, subject to no others. If a plan of action is successful and contributes to the defeat of the enemy, it is good. No other questions need be asked. This is a single-minded approach that shuts out all other considerations. All that matters is the quickest and least costly way to total victory and the utter defeat of the enemy.

Militarism has no patience with humanitarian objections to some actions in war. If the easiest way to eliminate a military installation involves inflicting large numbers of civilian casualties, then that is the way to do it. In modern warfare, military leaders cannot worry about what happens to non-combatants. For modern war is total war, and in total war there are no non-combatants. All citizens of the opposing country are our enemies, so, to speak of their "rights" makes no sense. Victory will come more quickly and more decisively if we put aside all scruples about how we carry on the battle. If torturing prisoners of war gets us needed information, then torture is permitted. If wiping out whole cities and heavily populated areas will bring the enemy to his knees, then we should do it. Whatever contributes to the safety of our own troops and the successful prosecution of the war is legitimate. That is what war is all about.

Two characteristics of the militaristic mind stand out: *nationalism* and *authoritarianism.* Nationalism is the doctrine that national interest and security are more important that all other considerations, including international and religious ones. It involves total, unquestioning devotion to the state and is best expressed by the famous slogan, "My country, right or wrong!" This supersedes all other loyalties, including those that come from religion. The nation's leaders are the supreme authority; they can be second to none. Persons serving in the armed forces must follow all orders without question. "Ours not to reason why, ours but to do and die." Civilians must support not only the war that the nation's leaders have declared but also the way those leaders choose to carry on the war. They may question the effectiveness of military strategy, but not its moral justification. If called upon to join the armed forces they must serve, regardless of any personal moral reservations. "Love it (the country) or leave it."

Pacifism

At the other end of the spectrum of attitudes toward war is pacifism. Pacifists reject violence as a way to settle conflicts, even those between nations. They see war as a great evil which solves no problems but only brings greater ones in its wake. When those who use violence claim that it is the way to peace, the pacifist replies that violence inevitably breeds more violence. It is ultimately self-defeating. The only way to peace is peace itself. This may involve sacrifice, even great suffering. But the price that is paid is never as great as that inflicted by war.

Many pacifists are Christians. They point to many of the sayings and actions of Jesus in support of their position. "You have heard that it was said to men of old, 'You shall not kill' . . . But I say to you that everyone who is angry with his brother shall be liable to judgement." "You have heard that it was said, 'An eye for an eye and a tooth for a tooth.' But I say to you, do not resist one who is evil. But if anyone strikes you on the right cheek, turn to him the other also." "You have heard that it was said, 'You shall love your neighbor and hate your enemy.' But I say to you, Love your enemies and pray for those who persecute you." (Mt. 5:21-22, 38-39, 43-44)

Pacifists oppose resorting to war as a way of settling international disputes. They reject war by refusing to serve in the armed forces. For them to take part in the violence of war would violate their most deeply held moral convictions.

Just War Theory

Those who are satisfied neither with militarism nor with pacifism prefer some form of what is called the Just War theory. They cannot accept militarism because it refuses to put any limit on what combatants may do in war. They cannot justify atrocities, massacres, and torture simply in the name of victory. They feel that there must be some limit placed on warmakers; otherwise even those whose cause is just may lapse into barbarism. To them, victory without honor is an empty victory. There are some things that must never be done, even in a just cause.

On the other hand, they cannot be pacifists either. They say that sometimes force must be used against unjust attacks, otherwise we fail to fight against evil. They fear that pacifism may encourage aggression, and that greater evil may result than if we had actively opposed it. So a nation has the right to defend itself against attack by an enemy.

The Just War theory has been part of the Catholic tradition for centuries. Unlike militarism, it places definite conditions and limits on the waging of war. It insists that war be declared only as a last resort, when all reasonable attempts at compromise and accommodation have failed. Since war brings such horrors, it must be clear that it is the lesser evil; i.e., that the consequences of not going to war would be even worse.

Once war has begun, there are limits on what may be done. Noncombatants must be spared as much as possible. Prisoners of war must not be tortured or killed. Any escalation of hostilities that brings on greater evils than the nation is trying to prevent, is forbidden. In other words, we are still held to basic standards of humanity and justice. These standards are admittedly very hard to uphold in time of war, when excesses and atrocities inevitably take place from time to time. But the nation is obliged to try, otherwise it loses all claim to justice in pursuit of its cause.

The Second Vatican Council endorsed this approach to war in one of its solemn decrees:

> As long as the danger of war remains . . . governments cannot be denied the right to legitimate defense once every means of peaceful settlement has been exhausted. Government authorities . . . have the duty to protect the welfare of the people entrusted to their care . . .
>
> But . . . the possession of war potential does not make every military or political use of it lawful. Neither does the mere fact that war has unhappily begun mean that all is fair between the warring parties . . .
>
> With these facts in mind, this most holy Synod makes its own the condemnations of total war already pronounced by recent Popes, and issues the following declaration:
>
> Any act of war aimed indiscriminately at the destruction of entire cities or of extensive areas along with their population is a crime against God and man himself. It merits unequivocal and unhesitating condemnation.
>
> *(Pastoral Constitution on the Church in the Modern World)*

This approach to the terrible problem of war seems the most reasonable to many people, but it does have its weaknesses. From one side, the militarists criticize it for being too idealistic, too impractical. They say that it is impossible to fight a "clean" war; the best thing to do is to take the gloves off and do whatever has to be done to gain total victory. From the other side, the pacifists also criticize it. They agree with the militarists that war always brings with it atrocities and indiscriminate destruction. But their conclusion is the opposite: since we cannot wage war in a morally defensible way, we should not wage it at all. For the damage we do always outweighs the good that we try to accomplish.

The Church, while endorsing the Just War theory, recognizes its limitations. So it makes a place for pacifism in the life of a Christian. Catholic pacifists are honored in the Church and are supported by Church leaders as being in keeping with Catholic tradition.

So there is room both for pacifists and for Just War people. Thus the Church teaches that service in the armed forces is an honorable profession, but it also defends the right of conscientious objectors to refuse such service in the name of conscience. This goes both for universal conscientious objectors, who renounce all wars, and for selective conscientious objectors, who decline to take part in particular wars which in their opinion do not meet the requirements of the Just War theory. This is somewhat different from American civil law, which recognizes the rights of universal conscientious objectors but not of selective conscientious objectors.

Militarism, on the other hand, is irreconcilable with Catholic teaching. So is extreme nationalism which makes obedience to the state (and to military authorities) the supreme law of conscience. "My country right or wrong" looks at first sight like simple patriotism, but it is really idolatry because it violates the First Commandment: "I am the Lord your God. You shall have no strange gods before Me." Loyalty to the nation must take second place to obedience to God's laws; otherwise it becomes a competing religion.

This is a difficult truth for some patriotic citizens to grasp. They cannot imagine having to choose between obedience to God and allegiance to their country. Fortunately, most people never have to make such a terrible choice. But the Nürnberg war crimes trials after World War II brought the truth home to thinking people. Defendants in those trials tried to justify their participation in the most hideous crimes against humanity because they were acting as patriots in following the orders of their superiors. In convicting many of these war criminals, the international tribunal stated what religious people have always known and should never have forgotten: that there is a higher law and a higher authority than that of the state. For Christians and Jews, that authority is God.

A Just Nuclear War?

The development of nuclear weapons, with their awesome capacity for destruction, has convinced many that the very idea of a just nuclear war is unthinkable. How, they ask, could we ever justify the slaughter of millions, the deadly effects of radiation, the threat to the very life of the planet? They conclude that nuclear pacifism is the only sane choice open to us. We must simply renounce, unconditionally, the use of nuclear weapons, no matter what the provocation. Some go even further. They say that since we may never use nuclear weapons, we should not have them in the first place. The arms race, instead of making us safe, makes the world an ever more dangerous place.

As we saw earlier, many are just as convinced that we need to stockpile these weapons and keep them ready in order to discourage any enemy from attacking us. In order to protect ourselves from possible nuclear blackmail, we must be at least as strong as any potential adversary. The enemy must know that if they attack us they risk total destruction of their own people. This is called the strategy of deterrence, and we have lived with it for almost half a century. Those who favor "peace through strength" insist that there is no other way to avoid the risk of nuclear war and possible catastrophic defeat.

The Roman Catholic bishops of the United States, during the decade of the 1980's, tried to come to grips with these hard questions and offer moral guidance to Catholics and other Americans. They studied the issues, consulted government and military authorities and experts, listened to advice from organizations of citizens and from private individuals. They invited criticism from all quarters and prayed long and earnestly for the guidance of the Holy Spirit. At last, in 1983, they issued a pastoral letter, *The Challenge of Peace*, addressed to church members and to all men and women of good will. It represents the official teaching of American church leaders on war and peace.

The bishops do not claim to have any easy answers to these agonizing questions. And they readily admit that intelligent people of good will can and do disagree on what political and military strategies can best insure lasting peace. Even among themselves there were disagreements. One group leaned toward the pacifist position. They wanted the hierarchy to condemn not only the use of nuclear weapons but even their possession. They wanted the country to move from reduction to elimination of nuclear weapons as soon as prudently possible.

The majority of bishops, however, decided to move more slowly. They reluctantly admit that our country may have to maintain a nuclear arsenal as long as the threat of attack or of an invasion of Western Europe persists. In other words, they agree to the strategy of deterrence known as MAD (mutually assured destruction). But they note that as long as we and other superpowers are armed to the teeth and on alert, this is not real peace, but "peace of a sort." And we should not settle for it. It is too unreliable, too dangerous.

On the actual use of nuclear weapons, they took a strong and uncompromising position. We must never use them under any circumstances. The consequences of nuclear war are so terrible, the extent of destruction so incalculable, that a Christian can never agree to be a part of it. It goes against every decent human instinct. It is utterly contrary to the reverence for life that is demanded by the love of God and neighbor that we profess. They went so far as to say that even if this nation were to suffer a nuclear attack, we should not respond in kind. And if anyone is ordered to participate in a nuclear attack or retaliation, he or she should simply refuse.

A noted newspaper columnist referred to the bishops' teaching as "an astonishing challenge to the power of the state." There are many Americans, including some Catholics, who will find this teaching difficult to accept. But as religious leaders committed to applying Christian principles to the problems of today's world, they could not have said anything else.

Finally, since the development and stockpiling of these weapons increased the risk of their use and do not contribute to a genuine peace worthy of the name, the bishops call upon the nation's leaders to make every effort to reduce and eventually eliminate nuclear arms through diplomatic negotiation. If such efforts are not made vigorously and honestly, the bishops warn, they will reconsider their qualified approval of the status quo. A nuclear stalemate, without any real movement toward reduction and elimination, is unacceptable.

For some, these are hard sayings. But the threat to human life on this planet is so grave that strong measures are called for. Indeed, many feel that the bishops compromised too much, that they should have taken a stronger antinuclear position. Perhaps. But they have spoken from conviction, after study, prayer, and dialogue. It is now up to each of us to do the same. There is no more serious moral issue facing us than this one. The stakes are higher than humankind have ever known. The price of error could be devastating in the extreme, not only to us but to generations after us. Each of us is called to do what we can to avert the ultimate catastrophe and to work for a just and lasting peace.

The Seamless Garment

When criminals were crucified in Roman times, the soldiers who used to carry out the executions would parcel out the victim's garments among themselves. Jesus wore a seamless robe that was too finely woven to be divided, so the soldiers who crucified him drew lots for it (John 19:24).

The Catholic bishops of the U.S. have presented their fellow Christians with a formidable challenge. They ask us to show reverence for human life in a consistent way, treating it as a seamless garment that should not be divided. This is not as easy as it sounds. If I am against abortion, do I also oppose the stockpiling and use of nuclear weapons? If I am against nuclear war, can I be consistent and oppose abortion as well? And if I can meet that challenge, what about capital punishment? Do I want to defend the right to life even of those who murder their fellow human beings?

Many of us would find it very difficult to oppose the taking of life in all three of these cases. Anti-abortion rallies attract many people who feel deeply suspicious of all attempts at nuclear disarmament. On the other hand, many activists against nuclear weapons stoutly defend a woman's right to abortion on demand. And in both these groups are numerous persons who insist that the worst criminals should be put to death.

This is not surprising. It is easy to love our own people, not so easy to love our enemies. Our hearts go out to the weak and the helpless, but we are repelled by the heartless and the cruel. Can we see in all persons, without exception, the image of God? Can we recognize, in the most unlovable human beings, our sisters and brothers for whom Christ gave his life? And if we do, how can we treat their lives as anything but sacred?

The Many Faces of Violence

"No society can live in peace with itself, or with the world, without a full awareness of the worth and dignity of every human person, and of the sacredness of all human life. When we accept violence in any form as commonplace, our sensitivities become dulled. When we accept violence, war itself can be taken for granted. Violence has many faces: oppression of the poor, deprivation of basic human rights, economic exploitation, sexual exploitation and pornography, neglect or abuse of the aged and the helpless, and innumerable other acts of inhumanity. Abortion in particular blunts a sense of the sacredness of human life. In a society where the innocent unborn are killed wantonly, how can we expect people to feel righteous revulsion at the act or threat of killing non-combatants in war?

". . . We must ask how long a nation willing to extend a constitutional guarantee to the 'right' to kill defenseless human beings by abortion is likely to refrain from adopting strategic warfare policies deliberately designed to kill millions of defenseless human beings. Since 1973, approximately 15 million abortions have been performed in the United States, symptoms of a kind of disease of the human spirit. And we now find ourselves seriously discussing the pros and cons of such questions as infanticide, euthanasia, and the involvement of physicians in carrying out the death penalty. Those who would celebrate such a national disaster can only have blinded themselves to its reality."

—*The Challenge of Peace,* Pastoral Letter of the National Conference of Catholic Bishops

A Pacifist Looks at War and Weapons

"People feel a need to be saved from all the things that frighten them, so we are susceptible to anyone or anything that promises to save us. We fear our enemies and believe our way of life needs protection. So we bow before our nation and its military might, which literally promises us salvation. We fear the Russians, and the Pentagon promises to save us, so we do what it requires of us, including our surrender of our faith.

"But the one whom we proclaim as Lord has some very direct and simple words that apply in this historical moment in which the danger and challenge are so overwhelmingly clear. Jesus said, "You have heard that it was said, 'You shall love your neighbor and hate your enemy.' But I say to you, 'Love your enemies and pray for those who persecute you'." (Mt. 5:44)

"For centuries, most of the church has failed to make Jesus' command to love our enemies historically specific. We have said, 'Love your enemies . . . unless they are Russian, Cuban, or Iranian,' or whomever the government identifies as our adversary at the moment. We say, 'Love your enemies . . . unless they threaten you.' And if they do, you are released from the command to love and you may hate, acting it out in any form necessary . . .

"'But what about the Russians?' continues to be the most commonly asked question when I begin to talk about the nuclear arms race. Even in the churches, the Soviet threat gets more attention than the words of Jesus. The question may indeed be the right one, but it is being asked in a tragically wrong way.

"What about the Russians? What about the Russian people and their children? What would become of them in a nuclear war? They are among the hundreds of millions of God's children whom we seem quite ready to destroy in the name of freedom, democracy, and national security . . .

"We American Christians have elevated our nation, our system, and our principles above everything else, even the survival of the world. National loyalty has preempted our loyalty to the body of Christ. We have allowed thousands of nuclear warheads to be aimed at millions of Christians in the Soviet Union, with whom we share a common faith and Lord.

"It is historical irony that there were Catholics on the bombing crew that dropped the atomic bomb over Nagasaki, the first and largest Catholic city in Japan, and that ground zero—the target chosen for the bomb—was the prominent Urakami Cathedral, in which hundreds of worshippers were killed. That day thousands of Christians, including three orders of Catholic sisters, were destroyed.

"Jesus never said that we would have no enemies nor that they would never be a threat . . . What Jesus offers is a new way to deal with our enemies, a different way of responding that has the potential to break the endless cycle of violence and retaliation that now threatens us all with ultimate violence."

—Jim Wallis, "Waging Peace"

9

Deciding with the Church

By now it must be clear to everyone that this book was aptly named. It is often very difficult to do the right thing. When questions as difficult as these confront us, we need all the help we can get. So it's good to know that when we are faced with such difficult decisions we are not alone. Help is available from our Church.

There are two ways to react when people offer to help us: Either "Leave me alone!" or "Thanks! I needed that!" Some people prefer to be on their own and resent any advice on moral questions as interference or as violations of their privacy. Others are grateful for assistance in making such important decisions about questions that can baffle the best minds. So when church leaders, the bishops with the pope, speak out on some important moral issue, they usually meet with two kinds of reaction. Some Catholics don't want to listen unless the bishops agree with them. Others welcome the guidance offered.

What many people don't seem to understand is that religious leaders *have* to speak out on moral issues, or they're not doing their job. Especially when people are treating one another unjustly, they must raise their voices in defense of the rights of others, especially the poor and the powerless. Sometimes this is clearer after the event, when we look back. For example, we read about the days when slavery was practised in parts of this country and wonder: why didn't the churches speak out more strongly against it? In later times when racial segregation was the rule, we are shocked to learn that some churches not only did not condemn it but were actually segregated themselves. Today most of the churches of South Africa speak out against apartheid, and we applaud their efforts. For they are teaching Jesus' law of love and reminding everyone—even those who don't want to hear it—that this law applies equally to everyone.

Remember Nazi Germany? The record of Christian churches during that tragic time was a mixed one. Some religious congregations and individuals took a stand against what Hitler was doing. Some were understandably afraid to oppose the government. And others gave him their hearty approval. That was a time when people needed clear teaching to help them form a correct conscience about what was going on in their midst.

At the same time, in this country, the churches failed to speak out against a shameful miscarriage of justice. After the Japanese bombed Pearl Harbor in 1941, our government interned citizens of Japanese descent in detention camps on the Pacific coast for the next four years. Loyal Americans were deprived of their homes, their livelihood, their businesses, and their freedom. It was an act of hysteria and racism at a time of national crisis. No one spoke out for justice at that time, to the shame of all Americans. The churches should have protested but were silent. In defense of them it can be said that they were as confused as everyone else. But it was still a failure of moral leadership.

Those are examples from the past. This book has dealt with several present-day controversial issues. All of them, in one way or another, concern the way people ought to treat one another. If the church is to preach the love of God and neighbor, it has to try to help people figure out just what love demands in these difficult cases. When people say, "the church should mind its own business and leave people alone,"they show that they do not know what a church is for. It is not enough for a church to conduct worship services and lead people in prayer; it is obliged to help people live in accordance with what they believe. Religion is empty words and dead ritual if it does not lead to deeds of justice and love. "I hate, I despise your feasts, and I take no delight in your solemn assemblies. Even though you offer me your burnt offerings and cereal offerings, I will not accept them, and the peace offerings of your fatted beasts I will not look upon. Take away from me the noise of your songs; to the melody of your harps I will not listen. But let justice roll down like waters, and righteousness like an ever-flowing stream." (Amos 5:21-24)

Who Should Teach?

But who are the church? Who are supposed to teach? Not just the pope and bishops, certainly. All Christians are called to teach by the witness of their lives—sometimes by words, more often by actions. We should all be ready to encourage, to advise, to warn, and even to criticize one another in love. But in this church some have the special responsibility to preach the word of God and to teach in matters of faith and morals. These are the bishops in union with the pope. They are assisted by priests and others who are involved in parish and school ministry. Then there are the theologians and other scholars who bring their own special learning and skills to the study of these questions, and make their scholarship available to all concerned.

When Catholics are faced with difficult moral questions they should use the assistance of the church. If there is some authoritative church pronouncement on the question, members of the church should use that teaching as the basis of their coming to a decision. For this is what it means to be a Catholic: that we do not form our values or make our most important decisions all by ourselves, without any reference to our religion and our church. We do these things as members of a community. And since our church leaders speak to these moral issues in the name of the community, we are obliged to listen to them and to make our decisions in the light of their teaching.

When we call ourselves Christians, we are saying that we are followers of Christ. What does this mean? It means that we try to look at the world through his eyes. That we try to live by his values. That we consider important what he considered important. If we are serious about this, then our whole way of life will be affected. It will show up in the way we think of and feel about people and issues, and in the way we act out those thoughts and feelings. If we are true followers of Christ, then at least most of the time we will treat people the way he did.

How do we know how he thought and felt and acted toward people? From the Gospel accounts of his life, from his words and even more from his deeds. So, for example, we read in the New Testament that he had a special place in his heart for the poor, that he was gentle and forgiving toward sinners. He tells us that we must be ready to forgive our enemies and resist the impulse to take revenge on those who wrong us. His moral teachings are very idealistic, and some of them go against the grain. Sometimes it can be extremely difficult to forgive people who have mistreated us or those we love. The natural inclination to "get even," to strike back at them and inflict pain, can be almost irresistible. But Jesus challenges us to be a lot better than we thought we could. Trying to meet that challenge is part of the following of Christ. "What would Jesus do in this situation?" is the key question that a Christian asks when making a difficult moral decision.

It is not always easy, however, to figure out what Jesus would say or do in some situations. As we pointed out earlier, the world we live in is a tremendously different one from that in which Jesus of Nazareth lived. He was a man of his times, a First Century Jew living in a mainly agricultural society in the Near East. He knew nothing of nuclear weapons, organ transplants, respirators, amniocentesis, intravenous feeding, surrogate wombs or *in vitro* fertilization. Some of our most agonizing moral dilemmas are the result of these advances in science and technology, and we cannot look to the Bible for explicit, detailed answers. But Jesus says a great deal about the basic issues involved—about respect for life and the sanctity of marriage, for example. It is the duty of Christians in every age to apply Jesus' teachings to new and unforeseen problems. This will often mean paying attention not just to his words but more to the spirit of what he said.

Applying the Principles

Take, for example, the question of capital punishment. Jesus never explicitly addressed this problem in the Gospels. He does, however, have much to say about respect for life, about forgiving enemies, about not seeking revenge, about showing mercy to others if we wish God to show mercy to us. "Forgive us our trespasses, as we forgive those who trespass against us" (Mt. 6:12). Many Christians, including most church leaders today, are convinced that taking the lives of criminals is completely contrary to the spirit of Jesus' teaching. But many other Christians, appalled by the horrible deeds of hardened criminals, do not see it that way. This is a question on which Catholics can honestly disagree about how Jesus would act.

Another example is the building and stockpiling of nuclear weapons, as we saw earlier. Even the American Catholic bishops could not all agree on this one. The sayings of Jesus repeatedly reject any resort to violence, even in the face of violence itself. "You have heard that it was said, 'An eye for an eye and a tooth for a tooth.' But I say to you, Do not resist one who is evil. But if anyone strikes you on the right cheek, turn to him the other also . . . You have heard that it was said, 'You shall love your neighbor and hate your enemy.' But I say to you, 'Love your enemies and pray for those who persecute you, so that you may be sons of your Father who is in heaven'" (Mt. 5:38-39, 43-45). A minority of the bishops who studied and prayed over this question agreed with Christian pacifists that the possession of nuclear weapons contradicts the teaching of Jesus. But a majority of the bishops, like a majority of the Catholic people, thought that having them just for self-defense could be justified under certain conditions. Another case of honest disagreement among intelligent people who take Christ seriously and try to follow him.

A third example concerns some ways of helping married couples to have children. A few years ago the Vatican published an instruction dealing with the many new ways of relieving childlessness. Such practices as the use of surrogate mothers, sperm banks and *in vitro* fertilization and artificial inseminations by third parties were examined and rejected as morally unacceptable. Two basic reasons were given for the condemnation. First, any intrusion by a third party in the process of conception and birth is a violation of the sanctity of marriage and the exclusive nature of the relationship between wife and husband. Second, children should be the fruit of the natural physical expression of love by father and mother, and not the result of some artificial technique.

On the whole, the Vatican document got a very favorable reception from Catholics and other Christians and religious people who considered these new methods morally objectionable. They agreed with the church leaders that though the intention of helping childless couples was a good one, the means employed were irresponsible and violated important family values. There was one point of disagreement, however. Many Catholics, including several reputable theologians, thought that an exception should be made in the case of *in vitro* fertilization by married couples who could not otherwise conceive. Two reasons were given. First, there is no third party involved in the process of conception or gestation, hence no violation of the husband-wife relationship. Second, although the technique employed is artificial, it is not necessarily unnatural, but simply the use of effective means to overcome sterility. Catholic moralists remain divided, unable to agree on how Christ's teaching applies to this particular case.

It is clear, then, that applying Jesus' moral principles to new situations calls for a large store of skill and wisdom. It is easy to make mistakes. That is why Jesus tells us to pray for the gift of the Holy Spirit. "I still have many things to say to you but they would be too much for you now. But when the Spirit of truth comes he will lead you to the complete truth . . . and will tell you of the things to come" (John 16:12,13). The Spirit is available to all members of the church, and in a special way to those who teach in the name of Christ, the bishops in union with the head of the church. Christ has appointed them the shepherds of his flock, to lead and guide his people.

The pope and the other bishops, of course, are human and subject to error. Being sinners like the rest of us, they have at times lacked vision or courage. They have sometimes failed to read the signs of the times or to provide the moral leadership that was needed. This should not shock us. Jesus said that there would be scandals in his church because it is a church of sinners that is always in need of reform. Despite all this, though, he says to Peter and the Twelve, "He who hears you hears me, and he who despises you despises me" (Lk 10:16). "Whatever you bind on earth shall be considered bound in heaven; whatever you loose on earth shall be considered loosed in heaven" (Mt. 16:19).

Not only are church leaders supposed to pray for wisdom, so that they may teach wisely. They are also to use all the resources of holiness and scholarship that are available to them. This means listening to theologians who bring their special skills to the task of applying Jesus' teachings to present-day concerns, and to the larger church, the ordinary men and women who try with the help of Christ's spirit to lead more than ordinary lives. All have a part to play in the difficult task of making Christ's teaching a vital force in the lives of individuals and in the wider society.

Disagreements Among Catholics

Unfortunately, this kind of cooperation doesn't always work out smoothly. Everyone knows about the divisions in today's church. Catholics disagree on a great many things, and some of the disagreements make headlines. What are we to think about these sometimes angry disputes?

At one end of the spectrum, some church members are appalled by the spectacle of public disagreement between some Catholics and their church leaders. They think that this kind of controversy should never happen. They believe that church authority should never be questioned. For some, the ideal is blind, unquestioning obedience, and anything else is a betrayal of the faith.

At the other end of the spectrum are Catholics who are not at all disturbed by controversy, no matter how it is expressed. They are very individualistic people who feel that moral judgements are purely private matters. Most of them tolerate official church teaching as mere suggestions that are not binding in conscience. A few resent any authoritative pronouncements on moral issues as unwarranted interference in people's lives.

The popular media, especially television and newspapers, call the first of these groups "conservatives" and the second group "liberals," and give the impression that these are the only two kinds of people in the church. Many of these writers have very little personal experience of religion and are not very well informed about Catholic beliefs and practises. If they knew us better, they would describe a third kind of Catholic, which is found in large numbers and goes about the business of making moral decisions in somewhat different ways.

Catholics in this third group try to take seriously the roles both of church authority and of personal conscience in dealing with difficult moral problems. They acknowledge the duty of church leaders to teach in the name of Christ, and they listen attentively and reverently to what they have to say. They find that most, if not all, of the time these church teachings coincide with their own best instincts. Even when the teaching makes them uncomfortable because it challenges them to pursue a higher ideal, they appreciate this kind of leadership and guidance. Their attitude is one of docility and receptivity, expecting good advice from their spiritual leaders and ready to give them the benefit of the doubt.

Occasionally, however, they have difficulty with the official decisions of church authorities on particular issues. The pronouncement may fail to reflect their own or others' experience. The reasoning behind the decision may be unclear or seem inadequate. Perhaps others in the church community, such as respected theologians who are experts on the matter in question, have found the explanation unconvincing. It may seem like a case where the teaching of Christ in the New Testament has not been accurately applied to one of today's problems. When this happens they listen carefully to the voice of conscience as well as to that of authority as they try to find the truth.

Realizing that they themselves are subject to error, they pray for the light of the Holy Spirit. As well as they can, they study the Bible, especially the words of Christ in the New Testament, to find guidance. They consider the teaching of the church in past history as it relates to the issue in question. Finally, they listen to other voices in today's church, not only of those in positions of leadership and of reputable theologians, but of laymen and lay women who take their faith seriously and try to live in a way that is consistent with it.

Only after they have done all these things do they draw their conclusions and make their decision. If they reach a judgement contrary to that of the teaching church, they do so reluctantly. But they realize that as Christians they are obliged in conscience to follow their deepest personal convictions. As long as the teaching is not a solemnly defined, infallible doctrine, they can remain in disagreement on this question and still be loyal members of the church in good standing. Meanwhile they should be open to further enlightenment from prayer and study and other members of the community, and be willing to change their opinion in the light of new understanding.

Accepting Responsibility

Some Catholics are uncomfortable with this way of proceeding, but it makes a lot of sense and is in keeping with genuine church tradition. We have always been taught that we must take responsibility for our lives. Religious leaders can help us form our consciences, and we are obliged to heed them. But they cannot completely take from us the burden of choice. As the Second Vatican Council reminds us in the Pastoral Constitution on the Church in the Modern World, "Conscience is the most secret core and sanctuary of a man. There he is alone with God, whose voice echoes in the depths. In a wonderful manner conscience reveals that law which is fulfilled by love of God and neighbor." The same document, which expresses the official teaching of the universal church, reminds us that "the church guards the heritage of God's word and draws from it religious and moral principles, without always having at hand the solution to particular problems," and that "the Gospel has a sacred reverence for the dignity of conscience."

This third group of Catholics that we have been describing is far different from those who are impatient with authority, uninterested in tradition, and determined to go their own individualistic way without regard to the conscience of the community. They are not spiritual "loners." They make an honest effort to combine the virtues of humility and obedience with those of honesty and adulthood. They gladly accept the guidance of church leaders with open hearts and minds, and dissent only when they have found grave, solidly grounded reasons for disagreement. Such disagreement is at most a sometime thing, not their habitual attitude. Their overall stance is one of loyal commitment to the church as a whole, to its larger vision and basic ideals.

Catholics need not face hard questions alone. They have the support of a venerable moral tradition interpreted by authoritative leaders who teach in the name of Christ. They do not all use that tradition or respond to that authority in the same way, and so they do not always speak with one voice or reach the same conclusions. But despite their disagreements they enrich their fellow citizens in the wider community by speaking out for justice and being examples of loving concern. And that is the way Jesus wanted it.

10

Issues That Won't Go Away

Even if, by some miracle, we could all agree on the difficult moral questions that have been treated in this book, there would still be a great many hard choices facing us as a nation. No matter how responsible and just we may be as individuals and as a people, there are still several broad issues that just won't go away. They are all related to the American way of life, and we will have to face them sooner or later. In some cases, it had better be sooner rather than later, because we may be running out of time. And our very survival may be at stake.

Although these issues seem very different at first sight, they have one thing in common. They all involve a clash between two competing values that are very important to all Americans: freedom and responsibility. They concern the way we do business, the way we express ourselves, and the way we enforce laws and punish criminals. If there were easy answers to these questions we would have found them long ago. Some of them are so vast and so complicated that we tend to put them out of our minds. Subconsciously we hope that if we don't think about them they will go away. But they won't.

The Ecological Time Bomb

Let's take the biggest one first. It concerns our freedom to develop industrially, to build, to harness energy, to manufacture, to master the forces of nature and make them serve us. For some years now we have been aware that such industrial development, if not regulated, can seriously harm and maybe even destroy our environment. Everyone knows about the ecological crisis, and many governments, including our own, try to do something about it. We have all kinds of clean air acts, laws against pollution, emission control regulations, and an Environmental Protection Agency to enforce them. Much has been accomplished, but much remains to be done. Agonizing choices are often involved. If we insist that an industry avoid polluting the atmosphere or nearby waterways, we may limit its production and profits, and thousands or even millions of jobs may be affected. If we protect wetlands and coastlines from developers, we may have to pay a heavy price in limited opportunities for employment and housing.

From time to time, spectacular disasters force us to think about these concerns. Incidents like the nuclear accidents at Chernobyl and Three Mile Island, the Union Carbide disaster at Bhopal, and the Exxon Valdez oil spill in Alaska make headlines for weeks and even months. But these are only the most visible examples of a global sickness that goes much deeper. Some of the most far-reaching ecological disasters are actually happening now but will not be visible for another generation.

Within thirty or forty years nearly all farmland from Kansas to Texas, from Arizona to Arkansas, will be wasteland. The Ogallala Aquifer, formed by sand and gravel deposits over a million years ago, is a vast underground source of water for eight Great Plains states. Recently the farmers in that area began to draw on this source of water for irrigation at a greatly expanded rate. Each year they take ten times as much water as the aquifer can recover. The short term results are increased production and profits. The long term result will be an environmental catastrophe that will leave those farmers' descendants in poverty and will have a disastrous impact on the nation's economy.

The ecological crisis is no longer a merely local or even national problem. It has reached international, even global proportions. Some experts think that this may be the number one problem facing humankind in the twenty-first century, and only international cooperation may be able to solve it. In the face of threats as big as these, we feel powerless. But the next generation and the one after that will either thank us or condemn us for the decisions we are making or failing to make right now. We are all in this together.

The Economy

One of the most disturbing developments of the 1980's was the dramatic increase in homelessness in America. Not since the Great Depression of the 1930's had so many of our neighbors been forced to live on the streets. And no improvement in this terrible situation is foreseen in the last decade of this century.

The poor have always been around and always will be. But they have usually been more or less invisible to their more affluent fellow citizens as they huddled in ghettoes and slums. Homelessness, however, forces us all to confront the ravages of poverty. The sheer volume of misery leaves us numb, feeling powerless in the face of so much suffering. If this were a poor country with limited resources, clearly unable to house and feed its people, we could perhaps resign ourselves to the cruel fate meted out to so many. But we know that this is a land that has more than enough basic wealth to care for all of us. The fact is that people are going hungry in the midst of plenty. These things have happened not during a depression or even a recession but in a period of relative prosperity.

There will always be some who try to blame the poor for their plight. They want to believe that no one who is willing and able to work has to go without food or shelter. They would like to chalk it all up to laziness. Although some of the poor may deserve this charge, no serious person believes that the widespread problem of poverty is as simple as that. Honesty forces us to confront the facts: that some of the poor are unable to work, that many more seek desperately for jobs but cannot find them, and that many of the working poor do not earn enough to obtain the bare necessities of life for themselves and their families.

As bad as the situation is in this country, it is far worse beyond our borders. Poverty is a worldwide problem of staggering proportions. As the 1980's drew to a close, there were over 800 million poor. Of these, 450 million were malnourished or starving. These mind-numbing figures conceal countless stories of human suffering. And they make us ask: why? Is the earth unable to support us? Does our planet lack the resources to nourish its inhabitants? Although some experts fear that, in the future, over-population may someday lead to a global crisis of undersupply, the present crisis cannot be so simply explained. Our world is capable of producing more than enough to meet the needs of all our brothers and sisters, but we lack the skill or the will (or both) to make resources available to those who need them most desperately.

Some have thought that the cause of all these inequities is greed and selfishness. Maybe if the rich and affluent were more willing to share their wealth with the needy, our problems would be solved or at least lessened. There is some truth here, but it is not the whole story. To be sure, if those who have more would share what they have with those who have less, it would make a big difference. But the roots of the problem go much deeper. If we are serious about finding answers and working for real solutions, we must examine the economic structures which we take for granted and tend to treat as untouchable. In our own country, is there something in the capitalist system that inevitably leads to gross inequities and to mass poverty in the midst of plenty? On the world scene, are there features of international trade, multinational enterprises, and economic delivery systems that condemn whole populations to inhuman living conditions without any hope of extricating themselves?

As the twentieth century entered its last decade, the breakup of international communism as we have known it seemed to be taking place. The economic system it spawned has been discredited in the eyes of its own peoples, and even its leaders seem to have lost faith in it. We would do well to remember how communism arose in the first place. It was an attempt to achieve justice and a chance at a decent life for millions of people who had no hope under the prevailing economic system. The fact that it has failed should not make us complacent. We have yet to find a system that works for the great mass of humankind. As the Roman Catholic bishops of the United States observed in their 1986 pastoral letter on the American economy, "No one may claim the name Christian and be comfortable in the face of the hunger, homelessness, insecurity and injustice found in this country and in the world."

Many who consider themselves hard-headed realists are impatient with this kind of talk. They say it's all very idealistic, but that's the way economic forces work; you can't do anything to change them. But this is not so. Economic laws are not blind forces completely independent of human control, like the laws of physics and chemistry. They are the rules of systems that have been made by people and can be changed by people. The economy should serve people, not the other way around.

What changes should be made? There are no easy answers to this question. We will need great stores of wisdom and skill to find them. The task is so complex that few people, even the best informed, want to try. But this much is clear: freedom of economic movement must be balanced by a sense of social responsibility. We Americans have always been justly proud that we live in a society where we can go as far as our financial skills, imagination and daring will take us. We thrive on competition, and we reward the winners. But we can no longer close our eyes to the dark underside of this picture. This issue, like the poor themselves, will not go away.

Freedom of Expression

One of our nation's most cherished institutions is freedom of speech. We value highly the free flow of information and exchange of ideas. When censorship has turned up from time to time, we have sooner or later always resisted it. Realizing that a democracy cannot survive without a free press, we have insisted on allowing all communications media—newspapers and magazines, books, television and radio, movies and stage—maximum freedom of expression. This includes the right to voice unpopular ideas, so that the majority may not tyrannize the minority.

No one who really understands what this country stands for wants to subvert this ideal of freedom of expression. But there is a dark underside here, too, that we will have to recognize before too long. The founding fathers knew that a price would have to be paid for this freedom in the form of some damage to society. They knew that some ideas, given free rein, would be harmful to individuals and to the larger community. But they were convinced that the trade-off was worthwhile, that the good would far outweigh the bad, and that in the free market of ideas the voices of justice and responsibility would most often prevail.

It is time to put some questions that almost no one wants to ask out loud. Is the price of freedom getting too high? Are the voices of justice and responsibility winning more than they are losing? Just how much damage is our society tolerating by its commitment to free speech? The mere asking of such questions is going to make many people very nervous, because it immediately raises the specter of censorship. This is a healthy reaction, because every generation of Americans has to fight the battle against the thought-controllers and book-burners who spring up like weeds from time to time. But we should not stop there. We should ask: are we, as a people, committed to responsibility of expression?

The question itself sounds strange. "Responsibility of expression" does not roll off the tongue as gracefully and easily as "freedom of expression." But think about it. Isn't it a law of mature, adult life that freedom must be balanced by responsibility? Isn't that what we try to teach children and teenagers? Well, if we really are a nation of grown-ups, can't we ask ourselves how responsibly we are using our freedoms, including freedom of speech?

So let's look at our communications media. Do they really keep us informed? What values do they impart to citizens, especially the youngest and most impressionable? What contribution do they make to healthy sexual attitudes and family values? To what extent do they trivialize sex, encourage exploitive behavior, and promote infidelity? How even-handed are they in treating divisive issues like abortion? How effectively do advertising and mass entertainment inculcate uncritical consumerism and greed? How many parents in this country are happy about the influence of television on their children? Is there a single network that would show a program in which these questions are seriously and dispassionately explored?

Freedom of speech is sacred in this country, and it should be. But it should not be a sacred cow. There is an old and respected saying that freedom of speech does not allow us to cry "fire!" in a crowded theater. The reason is simple: in this case, the right to say what I want is subordinate to the right to safety and security of those around me. So the uncomfortable question must be asked: are the rights of citizens being violated by what the media print and air and show? Do those who control the organs of mass culture use their power and their freedom responsibly? Does the status quo serve the best interests of our people? These questions deserve an answer. Just yelling "censorship" is not good enough. This is an issue that we're not supposed to talk about, but it won't go away.

Crime and Punishment

The questions of law and order and of crime and punishment are nearly always in the news, mainly because of the high rate of crime. The solutions seem to elude us not because we have ignored the problems but because of certain American values that are always in tension with one another. By our Constitution and our traditions, we expect our government not only to protect us and our property but also to respect our civil liberties. We want law and order, but not at the expense of freedom of speech and the right to protest peacefully. We insist on the rule of the majority, but we are also committed to defense of the rights of minorities. Not all governments are as sensitive to civil liberties and the rights of individuals, so not all countries have the same problems that we do.

This tension between our need to protect society and our commitment to individual freedoms shows up in various ways. The police and other law enforcement officials are supposed to do all they can to prevent crime and apprehend criminals, but must also respect the rights of the accused. During times of high crime rates this can be very difficult to do. Law-abiding citizens can become so resentful and desperate that they are periodically tempted to punish all accused lawbreakers harshly and indiscriminately. Often their complaints are well founded, especially when criminals who prey on them take advantage of the justice system and manage to avoid paying for their misdeeds. But we must never sacrifice the rights of accused persons to proper treatment and a fair trial, or we will become just another police state.

A similar dilemma confronts us in the war on drugs. How far should we go in testing people for evidence of drug use? Should we give up the right to privacy and freedom from unreasonable search and seizure? If we did, we would catch more drug users; but would this still be America?

And what about civil disobedience? How should we treat otherwise law-abiding citizens who in the name of conscience violate what they consider to be unjust laws? Consider a few recent examples. In the sixties, civil rights activists like Dr. Martin Luther King Jr. deliberately broke racial segregation laws and thus helped to change the face of this country. People who do the same thing in South Africa to resist apartheid are regularly applauded here. During the Vietnam war, anti-war protesters often engaged in non-violent but illegal actions in their campaign against what they considered an unjust conflict. And many young men refused to accept conscription in the armed forces. Some were excused as legitimate conscientious objectors while others were punished. Are there limits to loyalty? Can we respect the moral convictions of dissenters from government policy and still defend the nation? This issue was never really dealt with, and will probably come back to haunt us again the next time we get involved in an unpopular war. Finally, how should we deal with anti-abortion activists who non-violently break the law in order to defend the unborn from legal violence?

Problems like these are always going to be with us. They will continue to challenge us as a nation to find a right balance between the demands of freedom and responsibility. Every generation of Americans has to fight this battle anew, for it will not go away.

Some of the problems described in this chapter have not been faced, and will have to be dealt with sooner or later. Others are always going to be with us. They all arise from different aspects of the American way of life. We are challenged to confront them not only as Americans but as Christians. As Americans, we must address them in ways that are true to the best ideals of our country. As Christians, we must apply the standards of Jesus Christ and try to find solutions that are in keeping with his law of love. Being a good citizen and being a good Christian are not exactly the same thing, but we should be able to find ways to be both. That is the task we face as we deal, in the future, with the unfinished moral business of today.

This book was written to assist all Catholics, wherever they may be on the broad spectrum of membership. It is also addressed to other Christians and to all persons of good will, in the hope that they may be helped to find their way through difficult moral questions and arrive at loving, responsible decisions. We live in a time of great moral confusion. Not only are some of the questions new and baffling, but the disputing voices of deeply divided people make it even harder to decide. We have not tried to make these issues seem simpler than they are. But we started with the conviction that the teaching of Jesus Christ, heard within a faithful community committed to following him, can help us find our way. We hope that it has done that for you.